D1536981

'OUR LIVERPOOL'

by

Chris Shaw

Grosvenor House
Publishing Limited

This book is published by
Grosvenor House Publishing Ltd
28-30 High Street, Guildford, Surrey, GU1 3HY.
www.grosvenorhousepublishing.co.uk

A CIP record for this book
is available from the British Library

ISBN 978-1-907652-29-5

About the author

Chris Shaw was born in Liverpool in 1966 and gained a love of writing about football when his report of a match against Middlesbrough at Anfield in 1978 ('Boro Claim Heighway Robbery') won a junior reporter's prize sponsored by the *Daily Express*. Shaw later went on to work in journalism for 10 years before joining the Lawn Tennis Association as national press officer in 1999. He worked in other public relations roles in Manchester and Liverpool and is now a senior lecturer. He lives in Lancashire with his wife Lucia and two children. This is his first book.

Contents

1.

Introduction

It's one of the most commonly used platitudes in the game. "Our supporters are the best around." You hear it everywhere from Newcastle to Norwich and sometimes it is genuine; a welcome mark of recognition from managers, players and directors for those who sacrifice time, money and even relationships to follow their team.

Of all the fans in world football, Liverpool's have a better claim than most to this much disputed honour. For a start there are more of us than virtually any other club on the planet. Liverpool are one of a select band of clubs who are truly global, with more than 200 official supporters branches and a television station that attracts viewers from Merseyside to Mauritius. In researching this book, I saw a fact sheet on a website for USA Licensing Expo 2009 when Liverpool FC was one of the exhibitors. It placed LFC's support at 100m worldwide. (More conservative estimates from academics who specialise in the business of sport put the figure at 20m). Away fans at Anfield regularly ask "where's your famous atmosphere?" But even this putdown acknowledges the Kop's reputation for noise, creative banners and almost feral support on big European nights.

Those who follow this club range from the casual, replica shirt-wearing student in South East Asia who fell in love with the Liverbird after Istanbul 2005 and watches matches at all hours on big screens in sports bars, to the hard-bitten Scouser who got an education on the Kop in the 1960s and never misses a match. I met both types of supporter – and many others in between – while researching this book. I spoke to hundreds of fans, followed their debates on online message boards, read their letters to the *Liverpool Echo* and the monthly paper *The Kop* and listened to their contributions on phone-ins. I conducted about 50 interviews with people whose dedication and love for the team was staggering, even when it was least deserved, in the troubled 2009-10 season. Their stories, opinions and insights are what you will read. This is not a book about me, although I will offer my opinions from time to time.

So what's the motivation? After all, bookcases are already groaning under the weight of LFC literature. We have had players' memoirs, a whole library of work dedicated to the triumphs of Bill Shankly, Bob Paisley and Kenny Dalglish. Then there are the record books, trivia offerings, annuals, quiz books etc. Fans, too, have been prolific in publishing their stories of epic journeys to Rome in 1977, of Istanbul 28 years later and of the terrible spring days in 1985 and 1989 in Brussels and Sheffield when our whole faith in the game was shaken. The short answer why I have spent the last 12 months phoning, emailing, tapping away at a laptop and reading blogs at midnight on Saturdays was to understand just why we bother. Why we bother, not in the sense of asking why we pay £40 to watch a dull 0-0 or worse, but to really get a handle on the nature of our club's support.

I say "our" and the title of this book is no accident. I was born in Liverpool in the great year of 1966 (we won the league), went to my first match in 1973 with my dad (a 2-0 home win against Derby County) and grew up in the north Liverpool suburb of West Derby which is notable to any Liverpool fan for two crucial reasons – it was and remains the area where the training ground at Melwood is based and it was home to the club's legendary manager, Bill Shankly. It is a long time since I lived in Liverpool but over the years I have remained an enthusiastic and unapologetically biased fan. I have gone to the match as regularly as I can for as long as I can remember, about 15-20 times a season these days. Not bad, but nothing like the dedication I encountered in my research.

That research featured contributions from fans in all five continents, from ex-Liverpool footballer Steve Nicol, pop star/writer activist Peter Hooton and the respected journalist, Charlie Lambert, who is my colleague at the University of Central Lancashire. It also involved chats with pub landlords, supporters' club secretaries, fanzine writers, bloggers, web editors and Andy Knott who organises the mosaics on the Kop. I spoke to the hopelessly devoted and the disillusioned, people who backed Rafa Benitez to the hilt during the tumultuous season of 2009-10, and others who didn't rate him. I was lucky to meet Liverpool fans in bars in Shanghai and the United States and joined a group of fans who travel to Germany each year to visit friends who support Borussia Mönchengladbach. I tried in vain to find anyone who had a good word to say about Tom Hicks and George Gillett. I went to both Hillsborough and Anfield on April 15 2010 for a day I had been dreading but instead found inspiring.

To get things done in life sometimes you need a motivation, a kick in the pants to force you to do something you might have done years before. In my case the inspiration to write this book came at a funeral. About 24 hours after Liverpool beat Real Madrid 4-0 in the Champions League in March 2009, I was paying my last respects to my mate Stephen Rooney, who was just 41 when he died while working in Saudi Arabia. A book of tribute was passed around that evening. I didn't know what to write then, nothing seemed appropriate, but I did remember what Steve had said in Athens almost two years earlier. We were in Syntagma Square, mulling over Liverpool's 2007 European Cup defeat to AC Milan and talking UEFA, forged tickets and other matters. I remember casually remarking that Liverpool's support had changed so much since we each went to our first games in the seventies and it would make an interesting book if someone compared and contrasted the home town and the national and international support and looked at topics of concern for fans. Steve reckoned that it was a good idea and I was the man to write it. So here it is, dedicated to his memory.

Chris Shaw

Writelines2004@aol.com

2.

2009-10: Cancel the DVD Order

"This (2009-10) has been a bad season. That is very clear." **Rafa Benitez**

You sensed on May 2, 2010 that it was all over for Rafa Benitez and he knew it. Minutes after Liverpool's final home game of the season against Chelsea, the manager and players went on their traditional walk round the pitch to acknowledge the fans. Benitez looked preoccupied as he walked past me and fans near me in the Lower Centenary stand on his way to accept warm applause from the Kop. We were looking back now with Rafa, not forward. No one wanted to say this was the end but it felt as if it was.

Sure enough, exactly one month later the Spaniard was "mutually consented", leaving behind him a club in turmoil off the pitch. His reign was notable for giving us the most magical event in Liverpool FC's long history, the historic Champions League win in Istanbul in his first season 2004-05, but it was also remembered for arguments behind the scenes and a failure to end a 20-year league title drought. Even after he left, a sizeable number of Liverpool fans remained passionate defenders of his record and said they were bitterly disappointed to see him go. The announcement that Roy Hodgson would succeed Benitez was seen by some of the former manager's advocates as a managerial downgrade.

Now the dust has settled on Benitez's six years at the club, there appears to be a reluctant acceptance that something had to change. Jamie Carragher expressed this well after Liverpool began 2010-11 against Arsenal. Not wishing to criticise Benitez, Carragher admitted that a fresh approach was needed after the previous, wretched campaign.

The 2009-10 season was one of the most forgettable at Anfield for half a century. In early April 2010 I received a text from a loyal Liverpool fan, not given to knee jerk criticism. "I have had enough of this season. Unacceptable," it said. At the start of it, Benitez's critics were predominantly external. Many journalists and pundits had made their minds up about his management style long before and mocked him for his squad rotation and transfer policy, even when he was taking Liverpool to two European Cup finals and a runners-up spot in the Premier League, which he achieved in May 2009. But before that calendar year was out, the criticism was growing among Liverpool fans and it got worse as results failed to do the team justice in the first half of 2010. On the day after the 2-0 Chelsea defeat mentioned above, the *Liverpool Echo's* Dominic King wrote the club was "on its knees" and said it was "torn apart by internal civil war...crippled by debt... possessing too many players who are not good enough." And King was one of the more understanding Liverpool watchers in the media.

This book has not been written to dissect one season in Liverpool's eventful history, but what happened in

2009-10 could yet have long-term implications for the club's future. Much as we would love to, we can't ignore this season. Some feared the worst before the season when Xabi Alonso's sale weakened the squad; others pointed to the lack of attacking back-up to supplement Fernando Torres's goals. A 2-1 defeat at Tottenham on the opening day of the season was significant as it demonstrated Liverpool's defensive frailties and showed Spurs' genuine emergence as a challenger to our position in the top four. Then came the dreadful away results, the beach ball incident at Sunderland, Torres's knee operation which cut short his season, not to mention Steven Gerrard's loss of form and the failure of squad players to stake their claim. Most damagingly of all, Liverpool failed to finish in the top four and therefore missed out on the chance of competing in the Champions League. This was disappointing for the fans who had become accustomed to seeing matches against Europe's finest in the Benitez era and it was very bad news for the club's stressed accountants.

It was alarming to see Liverpool looking sorry for itself, careworn from underachievement on the pitch as well as financial uncertainty and boardroom intrigue off it. As fans, this is not what we expect or demand. This is the club with the reputation for landing top prizes and it just doesn't belong in the doldrums. Often in 2009-10, Liverpool's players looked ill at ease and incapable of performing to their potential. Long before the final whistle blew at Hull on May 9 the oft-heard question was "where do we go from here?"

By the time you read this, 2009-10 might just be a painful memory. We could be doing well, playing scintillating football and Tom Hicks and George Gillett may have taken their ill-gotten gains to the land of the free. Or maybe we might still be tearing shreds off each other in frustration on internet message boards. Either way, it might be a good time to listen to Jan Molby.

I remember Big Jan, our midfield maestro of the 1980s and early 1990s, once saying in a radio phone-in that any manager wishing to take over at a new club should insist on asking the owner or chairman: what is my basis for success? What are the standards that need to be achieved and can they be met? Is it staying up, keeping the club solvent, winning the biggest trophies in the game or stability and the odd big day out at Wembley? Molby surely raises a good point. Do we as Liverpool fans really know what constitutes success anymore?

In the late 1970s and 1980s, it was an easy question to answer. Success meant challenging for league titles, European Cups and all other domestic honours. Under Bill Shankly, Bob Paisley and Joe Fagan we knew exactly how to recognise success and we met and exceeded any reasonable targets season after season. Being banned from European competition after the Heysel tragedy in 1985 forced Kenny Dalglish's team to refocus its priorities, but the late eighties brought continued domestic success and some of the most stylish winning football ever seen at Anfield.

Between 1976 and 1990 there were only two seasons when we failed to win a major trophy, but in the following decade there were just two campaigns when we won anything of note before Gerard Houllier's successful first half of his reign and Benitez's tenure. Since the mid 1990s the trend has been for periods of disillusionment to be followed by sudden bursts of success in cup competitions and the occasional runners-up spot in the league. We threaten to make a breakthrough only to slip back into the pack amid complaints about the motivation of the players, the structure of the club and worries about the long-term future. Our managers often hit a glass ceiling four or five years into the job. This happened to Roy Evans, Houllier and Benitez while Graeme Souness didn't even get that far before he passed his sell-by date. Managers have been brought in to repair the mistakes of their predecessor and this works for a while until the pressure of expectation overwhelms them.

Many football watchers were strongly critical of Benitez when he was in charge of Liverpool. But my own complaint is that the fair comments of some observers (too many mediocre players signed, a dismal away league record and a lack of movement when Liverpool were in possession of the ball) have been overshadowed by crass oversimplification and comments that defy logic. In April 2010, journeyman striker turned football pundit Steve Claridge, a tedious character who seems to have friends in high places at BBC Sport, shot down a journalist on *Radio Five Live* for daring to suggest that Benitez had enjoyed success with Liverpool. Claridge dismissed Benitez's achievements and said that if it wasn't for Torres, the manager would have been sacked a lot sooner. There was no balance from Claridge, no acknowledgement that the Spaniard had taken Liverpool to second in the league the previous season. Nothing to remind us who signed Torres in the first place.

Of course, the likes of Claridge are a sideshow and what really matters is the state of the club and where Liverpool will be in five years' time – on and off the field. To get there, we need to have realistic targets and they need to be communicated honestly between the club and the fans, not a realistic prospect given the current regime. We have to follow Molby's Law and be very clear about what constitutes success at our club. Much as we dislike Chelsea we know what their owner wants – the European Cup. Manchester City behave like lottery winners, but they are aiming high even if they are not earning marks for their dignity. We know that for Fulham, a place in the last eight of the Europa League was a magnificent achievement and reaching the final was historic. For Stoke, Birmingham, Wigan etc simply being established Premier League clubs means they have achieved their objectives. Even Everton seem to know their place.

We remain the odd ones out because we will never see ourselves as just one of the pack. In the 20 years after we were last crowned champions, our fans went into each season sure that just one more push, one final piece of the jigsaw would see us retain our rightful place "on our perch", as Alex Ferguson once almost said. Politicians know they cannot get elected if they promise to put up taxes and Liverpool FC managers and chief executives appreciate there is no future in telling the fans to be realistic and not to expect the title.

When looking back on Rafa Benitez's tenure, he can be seen as a "yes, but" manager. Supporters of Rafa would claim that yes there were disappointments but look at the Champions League he brought us, the 86 points and runners-up spot and all this to a backdrop of chaos and mismanagement in the boardroom. On the other hand there are those who said, yes Rafa did bring us Torres, but Benitez's successes were more by accident than design and you can't blame the American owners for his chequered record in the transfer market, his team selection and his puzzling substitutions.

So your view of the Benitez reign may depend on whether you are ideologically pro or anti. Yes, he was responsible for some of the greatest nights ever seen at Anfield, but did his cautious approach prevent us from achieving more? Yes, he made some strange signings, including an injured player in Alberto Aquilani, who has since been shipped out on loan to Juventus, but he also brought in Pepe Reina, Javier Mascherano, Daniel Agger and the wonderful Torres.

The 2009-10 season was one of tribulation in the stands as well. The general annoyance at Liverpool's poor form often threatened to spill over as tempers frayed. This was shown in two incidents I saw in the Upper Centenary in January/February. During the Bolton game, fans were at each other's throats over the merits – or otherwise – of Lucas Leiva and at one point in the Merseyside Derby, a middle aged fan two rows in front of me, turned round and berated a fellow Liverpudlian for "not saying anything positive the whole match". There was a semi-comic moment then when negative fan argued his case by saying that he had been going to the match for more than 40 years and was entitled to his view.

"If you have been coming here that long you would have seen worse than this," said Positive Fan. "Remember when Souness was manager?"

This argument is never straightforward. Positive Fan is, of course, right that if you have paid £40 in the hope of seeing Liverpool win then getting on players' backs is counterproductive. On the other hand, Negative Fan would say with some justification that £40 admission fee should guarantee better football than we often saw that season, especially from players with big reputations. If they really are stars then they should act like stars and perform.

Not all Liverpool supporters speak with one voice as a quick glance at the online message boards testified. On the one hand there were the Rafa loyalists, the sort of people who once marched down Walton Breck Road to save his job and believed he was to be trusted implicitly. Then there were the Rafa sceptics who argued that he had "lost the plot" and was "past his sell-by date". Often the language on the message boards was vicious with each win or poor result seeming to offer ammunition for one side to claim they were being proved right at the expense of the other. Some claimed that the pro-Rafa fans were "deluded" and one internet poster wondered whether the Spaniard had hypnotised sections of the Anfeld crowd. Others, who were dubbed IRWTS (in Rafa We Trusts), hit back by reminding their critics that they were supporting a manager who had restored Liverpool's credibility as a force in Europe and at home. Many shook their heads wondering if it wasn't time to ask whether we were all still on the same side.

Benitez's critics were not slow to remind the manager that he had "guaranteed" Liverpool a top four spot in 2009-10. But as the season drew to a close, the *Irish Independent's* Dion Fanning noted how the boss was still able to generate enough loyalty from fans who bombarded journalists with emails saying the manager should stay. Fanning wrote: "It is customary for their loyalty to be applauded slightly patronisingly at this point before asking: at what other club would a manager be backed in this way?"

It is the nature of football that the game moves on quickly. Days after clearing out his desk on Merseyside, Benitez was taking on a new challenge in charge of European champions Inter Milan, which just happens to be one of Hodgson's former clubs. No wonder it is known as the managerial merry-go-round. Understandably, there were some Liverpool fans who suggested that if Benitez was as bad as his critics made out how was he able to walk into such a high profile job? A fan I spoke to in the summer of 2010 went round to the Benitez family home in Wirral to offer his best wishes and to pass on a banner that had been specially made. The fan was struck by how attached the Benitezes were to the area and to the club. The Benitezes showed their commitment to the area by making sizeable contributions to local charities, including to the Hillsborough families and Rhys Jones campaign.

The baton was officially passed on to Hodgson on July 1, 2010. The appointment received a mixed response from Liverpool supporters whose criticism often reflected deeper worries about off-field problems. A good man, intelligent and well organised; no fuss, dignified and able to grasp Liverpool's traditions, said those who welcomed his arrival. A flavour of the month character who is wrong for the club and whose lack of trophy wins is a serious disadvantage, according to the pessimists. Others went further and argued that Hodgson was a "yes man for the owners" which probably said more about how badly relations had broken down between board and fans than anything else.

Promising a "no bullshit" approach, Hodgson began his first season in charge at Anfield arguably needing a good start more than any previous manager. I heard him described as a "diplomat" and a manager Liverpool fans would not be able to warm to. Winning over sections of the Liverpool support was thought to be a tougher task than keeping Fulham up and taking them to a European final. National newspaper journalists responded well to the appointment, but that cut little ice with the more doubtful Kopites. It probably made some even more sceptical.

Hodgson was the first British managerial appointment at Anfield in more than half a century to have no previous connections with Liverpool FC and his critics will be worried that he is 63 and has a CV which apparently included sackings by Bristol City, Blackburn Rovers and United Arab Emirates. (Hodgson says his only genuine managerial sacking was at Blackburn). How will he cope under the intense spotlight at Liverpool FC? Could we look back on the summer of 2010 in a few years and recognise it as the turning point, the moment when our club really started to become second rate?

I am upbeat about the appointment of Hodgson as long as we recognise it for what it is. Given his age, a long tenure seems unlikely so we have to back him as a stabilising influence in troubled times, someone who can get things right at Melwood, improve confidence and fitness levels and attract one or two ambitious players with a point to prove who can make an impact – Joe Cole and Milan Jovanovic, for instance. Hodgson's arrival also gives Liverpool a chance to do some proper succession planning. LFC seems to be a club in need of a plan and this could offer the chance to groom a future generation of coaches/managers. Jamie Carragher seems a natural future Liverpool boss although how he might gain the experience required to take the hottest of hot seats at Anfield one day is another matter. In any case, would he want it?

Every man from Paisley onwards has walked in the shadow of Shankly. The seven men who followed Shankly have been custodians of a great tradition. All of them have won at least one trophy and they have all encountered pressure, stress, controversy and significant changes in the way Liverpool FC does its business.

Hodgson deserves our best wishes. He was a player of modest talent and a manager for 34 years before he got the call from Merseyside. But he is ambitious and he knows he has taken on a job that will define him for good or ill. After all, this is Anfield, Roy.

3.

Supporters all over the world – Liverpool's special branches

"To me it is almost a duty to watch." **Bob Kabli, Dubai**

It is a long way from the Dingle in Liverpool to Baku, Azerbaijan in Central Asia, but for one Liverpool supporter the world has been made smaller thanks to developments in satellite television and mobile communications. The Dingle was made famous outside Merseyside as it was the backdrop for the television "comedy" Bread and many years before that it was the birthplace of Ringo Starr. It was also once home to Steve Armstrong who left the banks of the Mersey in the early 1970s; one of many who went in search of work or new opportunities elsewhere. But like other exiled Reds, he took his football allegiance with him on his travels.

Almost 40 years later, Armstrong's passport shows the evidence of his globetrotting as part of his work in the oil industry which is crucial to the Azeri economy. He manages to return to the UK as often as possible – usually for European matches – but the worldwide appeal of the Premier League has made it easier for him to fill in the gaps. It is a far cry from the mid-1990s when he first went to Azerbaijan and couldn't even access BBC World Service.

"Back then you had to phone home to get the scores, but now we get more live Liverpool games than you do in the UK and football is one of the main topics of conversation," Armstrong said. "Part of the terms and conditions of the contract is that the Azeris who work for me support Liverpool! The Azeris like sport and they like to watch the big European games because their level and standard of football is comparable with third division in England. We have guys working in Kazakhstan, Malaysia and Siberia, but they have kept their membership up because they hope to come back. They are on short term contracts – anywhere between one and two years. If you look on the map, our southern border is Iran. We are still technically at war with Armenia who took lots of land. To the north you have Dagestan. Then you have Chechnya, Ingushetia and Georgia – all in the news recently – and right at the top you have Russia. On the other side you have Kazakhstan and Turkmenistan. It is a hot area. Unless you have a sense of humour and a good insurance policy you don't go there. We have a lot of people passing through who go on our website or we have worked with before in different parts of the world who make a beeline to get in touch with us."

Many of the supporters' branch people I spoke to admitted that patience and a head for administration were vital qualities. Armstrong takes a different view. "I don't have the tolerance for all that crap. I have been involved in British business groups and when you get the petty minded who come asking for stupid things they know not to bother asking me. They will go to another committee member so they will get more sense out of them than out of me."

Whether it is the 37 members of the Azeri branch or the much bigger numbers in Scandinavia, the model is the same for the 200 affiliated branches in all corners of the world. They generally adopt a bar in a city which shows all Liverpool's games, they have their own branch crest which is a variation on the Liverbird theme and a few of the keenest followers make an annual pilgrimage or two to Anfield. A trip to a home match is the equivalent of two months' salary for an Azeri and therefore out of the question, and the once a season treat is also major financial sacrifice for members of Liverpool's worldwide fan base who live in more accessible parts of the globe.

Across the Irish Sea, Liverpool FC can boast 33 official supporters' branches in Northern Ireland and a further 40 south of the border. For Leo Byrne, and his fellow branch members in Tralee, County Kerry, there are two big organised trips to Anfield – one before Christmas and one towards the end of the season. On these occasions match day starts at 2.30am with a coach trip to Dublin before making the connections to Liverpool. On the mainland we often assume that Ireland is just a short trot from Liverpool, but it costs the Tralee members 360 Euros when ticket costs and hotels are included. On one eventful trip a few years ago, the Tralee contingent came off the ferry in Ireland in the dark and had a breather on the coach, when they heard what they thought was a horn blowing. After ignoring it once, they became a lot more curious when they discovered they were parked on a freight train line.

Needless to say the coach driver decided it was time to make a sharp exit.

Byrne said: "It's like a schoolboy football team in that you have two or three who do all the organising. You do get the odd headache, like when you are waiting for 36 tickets for a European match and they haven't turned up a few days before. I suppose in Ireland most guys would support an English team. Who you support might depend on which Irish players played for that team or you might be influenced by who people in your family support. You get a lot of young kids who are attracted to a team by one player like (Fernando) Torres at Liverpool or (Cristiano) Ronaldo when he was at United. For me, it was watching (Steve) Heighway and then (Ronnie) Whelan, (John) Aldridge, (Jim) Beglin – those kind of players."

Dublin-based blogger Gerry Ormonde has seen big changes in the nature of support – with low cost air travel playing a significant part. "Going back to my father's time and my uncle's time they used to go over on cattle boats that would head to Holyhead first to offload the cattle before going to Liverpool. The cattle got all the best seats and I would hear all about the smells and how difficult the journey was. It would be 12-13 hours if there were no delays – and there were always delays. Even in the 1970s I would get a boat across on Friday night and it would take about seven or eight hours on the ferry and we would get to Liverpool on the Saturday morning. You fast forward to today, I can leave home at 10am on Saturday, go to see a game and be back on a Saturday evening. It costs a lot of money to do it that way and it is great. But what is missing is the camaraderie you used to get when you travelled across on the boat for hours.

There used to be an electrifying atmosphere which would come out at the game."

When I spoke to Riccardo Jansen before the 2010 World Cup, excitement was already building among the Cape Town branch of the Liverpool supporters. But, as big a deal as the global event was in South Africa, it seemed that what really mattered to this group were matters at Anfield. In a troubled season, it was a tonic to find out more about a multicultural branch in a city that has had so much to deal with in the last 50 years. Jansen describes his trip to Merseyside in 2006 as a holiday of a lifetime even though he saw us get knocked out of the Champions League by Benfica.

Back in South Africa, he and a group of fans have their own match day rituals that they play out at a favourite bar. "We get dressed in the home kit and come with scarves and decorate the bar with banners. We normally sing 'You'll Never Walk Alone' before the game and after the game. We sometimes have Scousers over here on holiday which all helps the atmosphere.

"I have been watching LFC since the 1980s in the days of (John) Barnes, (Ian) Rush and (Peter) Beardsley. That attracted me very much. There are a lot of older supporters with us in their late 40s, early 50s have been along for a long time. We had a place we used to go to in Cape Town called the Anfield Arms, quite a big place. We had 182 registered members. The owner emigrated to Australia and we had to find a new venue. Currently the venue we use now is owned by a Portuguese guy, Jamie Monxaica, who is a Liverpool fan. There are lots of Man U, Arsenal and Chelsea – the big four. But mostly the support is for Liverpool. Our games get first preference."

Those of us who have occasionally watched a Liverpool match when we have been abroad may enjoy its novelty value and we may recall being in a bar in a holiday destination wearing shorts and a enjoying a leisurely break from the heat of the beach. But for Liverpool fans abroad, fitting support for the team can be difficult given the demands of the day job and time differences.

Jansen reckons he sometimes spends six hours a day on activity related to the LFC branch. "Emails keep coming through and I have to reply to them. I even get emails from guys in Angola, Zimbabwe and we try to help them. I am happy to do it. I don't mind doing it. In Zimbabwe there are about eight guys and they are trying to set-up a branch over there. They watch English football, especially Liverpool, every game they get a chance to watch."

Like many LFC branches, Cape Town is active in charitable work, a fact that Jansen is rightly proud of. "We are there for kids. There was an email to the Jo'burg Supporters Club which was sent to us. This lady was unemployed and couldn't afford to send her kids to football training and we provided her two boys with brand new Liverpool kits – the latest home and away kits and boots. We were glad to help them. We are also involved in the Community Chest Twilight Team Run which is held every December in Cape Town. It is a charity event with companies in Cape Town and we felt it was a good cause and Liverpool supporters show that strong belief and if we can help we will help. It is a big walk (20k) and we all have fun together. We pay a fee as a team and the money gets donated to charity."

It is a similar story in Dubai where fans have been involved in raising money for the Marina Dalglish Cancer Charity appeals. Dubai gives another dimension of the true internationalisation of many LFC branches as in the oil rich emirate, expats from Merseyside and London rub shoulders with fellow Liverpool supporters from Syria, Egypt and Pakistan.

Dubai-based Red Dave Padmore said: "You are never embarrassed about Liverpool. Whenever you talk about football and the 'who do you support?' question comes along, you mention Liverpool and the recognition is there. Everyone knows Liverpool. There are only a handful of teams in the UK you can say that about. They can always name the players – Egyptians, Syrians are all football fans. I have travelled for 20 years and the sad part was always the amount of Man United fans. I used to dread going to bars because you would be trying to watch Liverpool and there would always be Mancs there. It was terribly frustrating. In the early years in Dubai I didn't watch Liverpool in bars because it didn't appear that there were that many Liverpool fans about. Then I found out about Dubai Reds in an advertisement in the paper. I went out of my way to hunt them down and I have been going to the Underground in Dubai to watch the matches and it has changed my perspective."

For Padmore, who is originally from Ellesmere Port, the limitations of globalisation were made uncomfortably clear on one occasion. "My lad came home from school one day and said 'Manchester United's a great team.' I opened the garage door and said 'you know where you will be sleeping? We'll move your bed in.' He took it literally and that was it and he realised then he had to be a Liverpool fan.

"That's the sad thing about living over here that we don't go to the games together very often. He has been to Anfield three or four times in his life. By his age, I had already done four full seasons and never missed a game. I watched 10 full seasons from 14 and I moved away at 24 and I literally didn't miss a home game and went to some away matches. What days they were."

Dave and his fellow branch member Bob Kabli are among up to 300 to 400 fans who watch their games in the Underground bar in Dubai and with beer prices the equivalent of £5-£6 a pint it is not surprising the regulars take advantage of 30% discount for their drinks. Kabli says that not only are 40 nations represented in this Liverpool branch but the mailing list ranges from a Saudi labourer to a sheikh from Qatar. "We did it almost in the Liverpool way. We didn't advertise it or heavily promote it. It was a case of if you want to join, feel free. It has gone from strength to strength and we have 200 paid members. It has grown beyond our wildest expectations and it is well established with the local media. If you watch a Liverpool match in London, people don't really talk or acknowledge each other but here it is like a college or a holiday and it is much friendlier. Every game is live here and in 2008-09 I went to every single one at The Undergound despite some being midnight kick offs and having a 7am start for work.

"When we lose we go home and have a grumble. But to me it is almost a duty to watch. We have had some great nights with fans who have been in Dubai and wanted to meet Liverpool fans. It is amazing when you see 50 people in the bar at midnight to watch a Champions League match. We try to get the singing going to replicate the Kop."

That last comment is supported by *FourFourTwo* magazine which described the passion in the Underground as the "closest atmosphere you will get in the Middle East to actually being at a live Premiership game".

Nearer home, the Aberdeen branch has a scheme where fans' attendance is monitored and those who watch all the matches in the pub are given preference for match tickets. This brings up the nice image of fans sending in a letter (or text, email or Tweet) to explain their "absence" from watching a match in a bar. The fans put an ad in the paper to tell other branch members they will be meeting in the Carleton. Branch secretary David McDougall said: "If we see your face every match in the pub we will mark you present, like a school register. It is like a loyalty scheme and it was one of the committee lads who came up with the idea. In the 1990s we used to get 50-60 tickets a game and now we struggle to get 20-25."

Jersey is another stronghold of Liverpool support. Like many branch secretaries, Paul Ashton, an exiled Scouser who was attracted to the island for its low taxes and quality of life, sees ticket allocation as a big issue. "We haven't been able to get tickets to away games for five years. These days I get to about two to three games a season, more if you take into account European matches. Our branch has Scousers, Welsh, Irish and Polish supporters and Jersey French fans – so there is quite a mix. Our fans are very keen on the souvenirs and merchandise and sometimes when you go to Anfield you want to be on the other side of the road! Some of them wear shirts with "Fuck United" – they don't care.

"Nowadays at the match you sit next to Scandinavians, Irish, fans from all over the place. They are all very keen. I think it makes for a good atmosphere. I am more laid back about supporting Liverpool now because of the telly and you can watch so much football on Sky. I am a bit of a coach potato when I have Sky in the house."

Like other branches, Jersey offers members the chance to meet heroes from past and present with events involving ex-players. For Ashton, helping to organise these events is among the most enjoyable work he does.

"We had a dinner in 2009 when Phil Thompson and the comedian Willie Miller came over. It was a fantastic night and Phil showed he was not just a great ambassador for the club but also for the town. We have also had Ian Callaghan and Roger Hunt here as well. To fans of my age, they were the players we associate with most, from the 1960s and 70s."

Of all the 200 branches outside Merseyside, the nearest to Anfield is Lancashire. In this part of the country, fans have their pick of teams to follow, but Liverpool has long been a well supported club in the Red Rose County. Martin Trotter, who has been connected with the branch since 1999, said: "Even through this drab period of not winning the league there is still strong support for Liverpool. There are probably as many Liverpool fans in Preston as Preston North End fans. When you leave that stadium (Anfield) it is like leaving no other place, especially after a big European night. The only other feeling I would compare it to, was leaving the old Wembley when we had won a cup.

"We had family in Birkenhead and they used to go and watch Liverpool when Billy Liddell played for them. I took on Liverpool through my father. I went to the Cup Final in 1971. We used to have buses going from Kendal and when I was old enough in 1972/73 we used to get the bus and walk down Scottie Road to the ground."

Trotter's story is a familiar one. All over the world, family connections, famous players from the past, and the magic of Istanbul have inspired fans to join the community of Liverpool supporters. The level of commitment is astonishing and often humbling. For these fans 'You'll Never Walk Alone' is as much a philosophy as a song.

4.

Media, fanzines and blogs

"We don't tend to switch off. We are permanently looking for news on Liverpool and something about a player, something we might be interested in." **Gareth Roberts, writer, blogger and Liverpool fan**

Imagine for a moment that we went back in our football Tardis to 1970, taking our media with us. It's February 21 and Liverpool have just lost an FA Cup sixth round tie at Watford. The Saturday night phone lines to BBC's 6-0-6 and talkSPORT are jammed with irate callers. First up is Dave from Pontefract.

"Hello, as I was saying to your researcher, I love Shanks but the fella has lost the plot. He has done a lot for us but he has got to go. If you're listening, do us a favour, Shanks, step down. I would like the board to get a good manager like Malcolm Allison, someone who can take the club forward. We have won nothing for four years, don't score enough goals when it really matters and too many players are past it. Shanks has bought badly and we will never win anything with him in charge. It gives me no satisfaction in saying this…"

Followers of Liverpool's history will immediately recognise the significance of the match mentioned above. It is referred to as the landmark defeat that persuaded Bill Shankly to finally break up what was left of his celebrated sixties team and start again with younger players like Ray Clemence, Larry Lloyd, Steve Heighway and Kevin Keegan. It took three more years for the formula to work, but Shanks got there in the end. He learned from his mistakes, grafted even harder – no mean feat for a workaholic – and won three trophies in his last two seasons in charge. The legend was established.

So there was no Dave from Pontefract in 1970, no media campaign and no opportunity for fans to grumble. Partly that was out of respect for Shankly who was revered in Liverpool. Had fans been calling for his dismissal, others would have soon shot them down. But nowadays the landscape is unrecognisable. It sometimes feels as if we live in a 24-hour Sky Sports News bedlam where every scrap of information, each morsel of speculation is pounced on by the fans who comment and further fuel the constant chatter. The modern fan has never had so many ways of finding things out with so many news organisations hunting information of all sorts. The sports media is always hungry for more of everything – good news, bad news, speculation of all kinds to pass on to the fans. And Liverpool supporters are among the keenest to know exactly what is going on at their club as it happens and preferably before. The internet, message boards and rolling news provide the machinery to get it all to us.

One man who is better qualified than most to comment on the media is Charles Lambert who has covered football on Merseyside for 38 years with the

Bootle Times, the *Liverpool Echo* and the BBC. What does he think of the phone-in, for example? A good way to air opinions or an invitation for know-alls to spout rubbish?

"I think they are great," Lambert said. "They are entertaining and they are not supposed to be Encyclopaedia Britannica. If some dummy comes on and doesn't know what they are talking about we all have a good laugh. It is fantastic that the fans can interact so quickly with presenters that they get their opinions on air and you hear their voices as opposed to just reading a text. If you can hear their voice you can hear the passion or the anger. Yes, sometimes you hear someone who makes you want to tear your hair out, but why not? It would be awful if all we listened to was something we agreed with all the time. There would be no point in tuning in. The majority of fans are informed because they live and breathe the fortunes of their football club. They might not come from the same standpoint as another group of fans or another individual fan because everyone is different, but they all have a point of view.

"That is one of the great challenges of being a sports journalist. You are communicating with a really knowledgeable target audience because they probably know more about the club than most general football journalists. The fans live and breathe it every day whereas a journalist is probably covering a number of different clubs and sports."

Lambert recalled how arguments over team selection and tactics on Merseyside in the 1970s and 80s might develop slowly over several months. But does the instant reaction of 21st Century journalism lead to "knee-jerk reactions and they haven't been thought through?"

John Pearman who edits the fanzine *Red All Over the Land*, thinks so. Since the demise of *Through the Wind and Rain*, RAOTL and *The Liverpool Way* have provided a platform for fans who want to see their views in print. A typical issue of RAOTL (the 153rd edition was on sale in August 2010) sells 1,500 copies and campaigns for Liverpool values – respect of traditions, remembering our history etc. The editor admits his readers have been around a bit and don't like excitable sports broadcasters spouting opinion, courting controversy and asking: "Liverpool fans, what do you think?"

There is a healthy scepticism of "paper talk" on Merseyside and a feeling that shouting your mouth off in print or on the airwaves is never a good idea. Traditional fans remember Bob Paisley barely being able to string a sentence together despite bringing success that has never been seen before or since. Sky Sports News, with its ticker and breathless reporting, is of its time, but its bold, brash approach is not to everyone's taste.

Pearman said: "In the fanzine I wrote that a bad result for Liverpool is good news for *Sky Sports News* because it gives them another day to slag off the club. There are too many people who just want to knock. These are people who go on the phone-ins. They wouldn't know Anfield if it fell in their back garden. They just think 'I am going to ring up tonight and I will get on *6-0-6* or whatever.'

"They have these polls...I could throw things at the screen. That's why I don't listen to phone-ins because you do get the ill-informed fan."

RAOTL's disenchantment goes deeper than *6-0-6* and Pearman believes fans' publications like his gives a chance for LFC to be closely scrutinised. "The main aim now, as opposed to when we first started, is to try and get a message across to people that the club isn't open any more. They only tell you the good news and what fanzines try to do is show the other side and say 'look there are problems here'.

"If you read the (match day) programme and we get beat there is a happy message being promoted. On *LFC.tv* they will tell you that a player has signed a new contract; they are not saying someone has turned one down. Then you get a player like (Andriy) Voronin who says his ambition is to play for Liverpool when I don't know anyone who supports Liverpool who wants him to play. The club are trying to put over a 'happy, happy' image and it is not like that. Football has gone down a road where it has sold its soul to TV and it has now gone further and further down that road to a stage where there is no turning back. I think what fanzines do – and those of other clubs – is say 'look this isn't our game anymore. It is somebody else's game now. We were the reason the club existed and Bill Shankly used to call the Liverpool crowd a brotherhood. We are no longer part of the football club. We are just incidental. TV runs football. Fanzines say 'we know we won't claw it back but at least we will stay true to our roots'".

Lambert understands that there is a new kind of pressure on reporters compared to the days when he had to fill column inches in the *Liverpool Echo*. He has seen how much more difficult it is for journalists operating in 2010 to deal with Liverpool Football Club than it was for him in the 1970s in the days before press officers and news management by commercially savvy Premier League clubs.

"I can sympathise with football clubs that they have a vast worldwide media clamouring so they have to control them," he said. "When I covered Liverpool and Everton for the *Echo* I basically had free access to Melwood and Bellfield. I could go down and wander into the headquarters, didn't have to make an appointment, pretty much talk to who I wanted to. At Melwood, I could go down and watch the lads finish training. If Tom Saunders was there he would probably take me inside and make a cup of tea. We would have a chinwag. If there were players doing rehab in the gym I could just wander in and have a chat with them. If I wanted an interview I could ask a player directly and they would say yes or no. But these days you can't do that, can you? One of the spin offs is players don't have any concept of that element of communication with the supporters. I used to play squash with one of the Everton players on a regular basis, but these days because footballers are in a different sphere economically I just can't see that happening. So you don't get that connection and you don't get that understanding from reporters of what's going on in the football club. You don't know who is fighting who and if that is known it becomes a big headline. I used to see things going on and it just wasn't worth reporting. It was no big deal. We don't have the depth of coverage now and there is nothing reporters can do about it. It's just the way it is and we just have to live with it."

Lambert sympathises with the *Liverpool Echo* journalists who have to tread a fine line in covering LFC. Play it too critical they get no access to players, managers and stories, play it too soft and they lose credibility with their Scouse readers who have always had strong opinions on football.

"The player and the manager and (LFC's) media department headed by Ian Cotton are, I think, more likely to encourage a good relationship with the local reporter because it is important to the club that they are portrayed in a positive light in Liverpool. The reporter is under a certain amount of pressure to portray the club in a positive light because if he is constantly putting out a torrent of negative stories, the relationship with the club is going to suffer and the day to day access is obviously going to disappear. So it is a very difficult balancing act. I thought it was really significant the way Chris Bascombe (formerly of the *Liverpool Echo* now with the *News of the World*) played his coverage of the closing days of the (Gerard) Houllier era. Long before the end of Houllier's last season, you could sense that Chris had decided that he was not going to be seen to buttressing a manager who clearly was losing the plot. For several months before Houllier left, Chris's coverage became a lot more strident and a lot more critical than it had been up to that point. So sometimes it's a difficult call for a reporter and having been in the position of the lads it's one I don't envy. I thought both Chris and Tony Barrett (Bascombe's successor at the *Echo*) did a fantastic job and they did create a unique brand of coverage for Liverpool for themselves."

Like many other journalists, Lambert is active on the blogosphere as well as the traditional media. Liverpool is well served for thoughtful and incisive online content written for fans who think and write critically about matters at Anfield. Recent tribulations on the field and in the boardroom have given plenty of ideas to Gareth Roberts, who comes from Steven Gerrard-land in Huyton and blogs on *Well Red*. In 2009-10, he launched a print publication of the same name which features thought provoking articles from writers on a range of matters from the club's youth policy to ticketing arrangements.

Roberts said: "When I first started the blog I didn't expect anyone to read it. I did it for myself really and hopefully as I have gone on, the content has improved. I have decided to make it look a bit better as well. Slowly but surely, people have started to read it. At first I thought I would dip into it now and again and write the odd piece. I almost told my own story really...why I support Liverpool. Now it's more an analysis of games or situations. Often I wind myself up by reading all the forums and go on my own blog and vent what I think."

In researching this book, I have regularly been surprised at the scope and detail of comment and debate on all matters Liverpool. Often the debate can be vicious and sometimes it is adds more heat than light, but Roberts believes the online chatter shows how much so many care about matters at Anfield.

He said: "I know a lot of fans from other clubs and I think when I look at them they are almost passive towards the club. They tune in for the Saturday and watch the match and turn off again the moment the game has finished and move on and do something else. Liverpool fans and myself and my friends don't tend to switch off. We are permanently looking for news on Liverpool and something about a player, something we might be interested in. We feel as if we own the club in a way and I think that's why the ownership situation stirred up such a response because people feel wronged by what has gone on. It's not the Liverpool way and so on. That is why there is so much online and there are so many people talking about it. One of the reasons why there is some much happening online is because of the nature of the club itself."

Roberts admitted he was taken aback when he realised that 48,000 fans were readers of his blog, more than the capacity of Anfield. His opinions on Xabi Alonso's departure from Liverpool in 2009 saw an increase in traffic and Roberts is active on Facebook and Twitter. He is very much the model of a modern Liverpool fan, articulate and with perceptive views on the game and his club.

Rafa Benitez had a lot more on his mind than the internet when he arrived at Liverpool in the summer of 2004, but he was the first Liverpool manager to deal with the full force of Web 2.0 and user generated content. What this all means is that all us can be publishers, writers and producers. We can blog, post on message boards, upload our opinions by video on to YouTube or instantly slag off the comments of other fans, journalists etc. By the end of his last season in charge of Liverpool, criticism of Benitez had long "gone viral".

Merseyside fans branch secretary Les Lawson also sees much of what he calls the "Sky Sports effect". This involves "expert opinion" being used to support prejudices and Andy Gray, once of Everton and never a Kop favourite, is the prime target, but many other Liverpool detractors have recently been lining up to take pot shots, according to Anfield regulars. Paul Merson, Jamie Redknapp, Perry Groves and Stan Collymore, were all among Benitez's arch critics long before the Spaniard left the club. Redknapp was taken to task by internet posters and Rafa himself for suggesting that the big difference between Liverpool's 4-1 win at Old Trafford in 2009 and a 2-1 defeat a year later was that Alonso wasn't there to spread passes around. Redknapp was heavily criticised for not checking the team sheet from 12 months earlier when the Spaniard was also missing.

Redknapp's poorly researched musings were of particular interest to freelance writer Paul Tomkins who has the Marmite affect on Liverpool FC fans. A former semi-professional footballer who has written a series of LFC books and publishes views on his subscription website *Tomkins Times*, he divides opinion among supporters in a Benitez-like manner. This is probably no coincidence as Tomkins was one of Benitez's staunchest supporters and was granted a four-hour audience with the Liverpool manager at Melwood in the autumn of 2009. *Sunday Mirror* columnist Michael Calvin attacked Benitez for spending so much time with a "star struck blogger" but many of Calvin's newspaper colleagues were probably jealous that Tomkins got so much access.

Unlike some enthusiastic amateurs in cyber space, Tomkins is a capable writer who doesn't make loaded statements without backing them up. In another life he would make a good lawyer, using forensic investigating skills and a stack of evidence to make his points. Although you could disagree with much of what he writes, he had valid points to offer about the restrictions that Benitez had to work under and he rightly questioned those who jumped to conclusions about the manager without looking at the bigger picture.

Often it was easy to disagree with Tomkins' narrative and it was suggested that he could be too soft on Benitez, with a ready explanation for every one of the Spaniard's failings.

Tomkins is basically a fan, like all of us, just better connected and handier with a turn of phrase than most.

Yet in December 2009, he defended himself against critics who compared him with Nazi propaganda chief Joseph Goebbels. "It's not that it insults me," Tomkins wrote. "I'm guessing it is just too out there to be considered libellous – but it insults all those who suffered at the hands of the Nazis." Tomkins maintains that his motivation is to correct misinformation about Liverpool FC and simply wants to improve the quality of debate regarding the club.

Believers in the power of the internet to do good and the importance of online discussion in changing the way we follow Liverpool FC might see the *KopTalk* debate as a cautionary tale. For about 10 years a website called *KopTalk* has published "insider news" to subscribers detailing stories around Anfield and Melwood. For Liverpool supporters hungry for every last scrap of information, a site with well sourced stories that the national and local press couldn't get was surely a must. The site's editor Duncan Oldham duly built a loyal following of subscribers.

Things soured when fans left the website and set up a breakaway blog called *KopTalk Insider*. The rebels wanted to "expose" *KopTalk* and produced a long list of allegations which included ripping off fans, cyber bullying, producing racist content and supporting *The Sun* newspaper. In his defence, Oldham says he is a "proud father of two" who is always up for a laugh and remains positive despite "smears" from those he describes as rivals or fans that, it is claimed, have been banned from the *KopTalk* site.

For others, the internet offers the chance to be mischievous and wind up rival fans. This also brings serious risks; just ask Steve Sinatra. This unlikely named

Chelsea supporter, who lives in Australia, joined T*he Liverpool Way* message board in the aftermath of his side's 2-0 win against us in 2009. He posted some crude abuse at Liverpool, calling us "scum" and targeting Fernando Torres in a clumsy manner, known as "trolling". It is the modern equivalent of running into a rival fans' terrace and provoking their fans into a fight. If Sinatra was spoiling for a reaction he got it with a vengeance as within 25 minutes of his outburst, email details and an IP address were revealed and the first Photoshopped images in various sexual poses of him were shared. A Facebook group was launched offering followers the chance to "Punch Stephen Sinatra" with a digital boxing glove. This invitation was taken up more than 200,000 times and there were three days of trial by message board and more than 600 responses to his original posting before the moderator decided: "I am closing the thread, as the lad has suffered enough now." It showed there really is no hiding place online and that web users can be cruel, whatever their allegiance.

For some, this is all too dark. Whatever happened to humour, the game being about opinions and people putting it all into perspective? It is therefore a relief that Irishman Gerry Ormonde is around to lighten the mood with his witty offerings for *Kopblog* on *This is Anfield*. Something of a blogging veteran – he has been posting since the Houllier era – Ormonde has won awards for his regular articles on all matters Red. Ormonde has gained a sizeable following, mostly he admits, among international supporters. His posts regularly get more than 400 responses which is massive when you consider the *Liverpool Echo's* most commented on LFC stories struggle to get 100.

Like RAOTL, Ormonde worries about the demands of 21st Century football supporters. "Some go really over the top and you get it at all times, particularly more so with modern kids. Everything has to be instant and if it isn't they throw their rattles out of the pram. I do deliberately try to get humour in where I can. Before I blogged I read a lot of stuff that didn't appeal to me – people taking themselves too seriously. Sometimes when I read my work back I think 'I should have put another one-liner in there.' Let's not take it too seriously. Liverpool is important but let's have a laugh from time to time.

"What came back to me from the people who voted for the blog when it won the awards, was they were looking for something that was humorous, informative and well-written. I get some (emails) that make me laugh. I got one from a guy who said his daughter had written a song about Fernando Torres in his first season and could I arrange for the Kop to sing it at the next game because he and his daughter will be watching on TV."

Journalists like Lambert accept that behind all this there is a battle raging for influence and authenticity online and offline. He argues that like all Premier League Football Clubs, Liverpool will allow its fans full reign to express their views on their own blogs – as long as the official communication is done on their terms.

"The biggest change I expect to see is increasing control by the clubs," Lambert said. "More and more supporters are going to be directed towards the clubs' own platforms. Already we have *LFC.tv*, Liverpool's own website, we have a whole media department and clearly part of the remit is to project the club in the most positive light. I am a little fearful as to how much this is going to encroach on independent coverage of the club. Will the day come when managers' press conferences are only available via Liverpool FC's own outlets? We are heading that way already with some clubs and organisations. Are we going to see the day when newspapers are being charged substantial fees to send reporters? I feel that could well happen and the way the newspaper industry is at the moment they don't have financial clout. My fear is that authoritative, probing, trustworthy coverage of football is going to be at a premium. Not next season, but certainly looking ahead over a few years. What we are going to get is a sanitised version which purports to be journalism but isn't really. And when that happens the consequences might be some amazing fragmentation of the electronic media that we have now and that fans' own websites might start to become more robust and more challenging than they are now. How will they make money out of that? I don't know. The media is in such a state of flux at the moment with the local media losing money in a horrendous way. The future for media coverage of football is very worrying and the critical consumer is going to be short changed within the next five to 10 years."

Shankly and Paisley didn't have to contend with this brave new world where fans from across the world can trade opinions and insults about each other and their team's managers, anytime, anywhere. Shankly used a trusty old typewriter to reply personally to fans who corresponded with him. Could we really see traditionalists like Shanks or Paisley joining Facebook groups, updating their online profiles and checking out YouTube if they were around now? And how would Ryan Babel's outburst on Twitter when he was dropped at Stoke last season have gone down with Liverpool's celebrated managers?

"It is too much of a cliché to say that Shanks and Bob wouldn't have had anything to do with this generation," said Lambert. "Shanks, Bob and Joe Fagan were fantastic managers because they managed according to the pattern and the requirements of the time. If those people were managers today, does anyone seriously try to suggest they would not be clever enough to adapt? Of course they would. Times change and Bill Shankly, with his fabulous motivational qualities, would still be a terrific manager today. He would lay down the rules and he would make sure the players stick by the rules. One way they have of coping with it is to have a whole battery of media managers who look after these things and keep the media at bay. In my time I have been there when this didn't exist at all to now it having a stranglehold. If Ryan Babel was stupid enough to say something on Twitter when Shanks or Bob were his manager he probably wouldn't be the right sort of player for Liverpool and I very much doubt if either of those managers would have signed Ryan Babel in the first place."

5.

Ich bin ein Scouser

"A lot of Germans are like Scousers. They love football, beer and a good laugh." **Didi Hamann, quoted in the Liverpool Echo**

It's April 2010 and a group of Liverpool fans are standing behind the goal, arms aloft saluting a memorable strike. It has got everyone applauding and bouncing. But this time we are not on the Kop, it is not Torres or Gerrard the fans are cheering. For one day only they are pledging their allegiance to another – Borussia Mönchengladbach and their promising young midfielder, Marco Reus who has just given his side the lead against Bayern Munich in a Bundesliga match.

As we will see in this chapter, fans of Liverpool and Borussia go back a long way and have developed strong and friendly connections. The highlight of these links is the football supporters' exchange visits which takes place twice a season. Fans from Mönchengladbach, which is a football hotbed in Germany near the Dutch border, take in a match at Anfield in the winter and the hospitality is returned each spring when Liverpool supporters hit the low cost airline trail. The calendar year 2010 was even more notable as the two clubs also organised a pre-season friendly in Germany which was a sell-out and saw the home side win 1-0.

The two trips are described as "friendship visits" and they live up to their billing. The Germans not only enjoy the experience of watching Liverpool play in the Premier League but they visit the bars of Mathew Street and immerse themselves in Beatles culture. The Reds go out to enjoy a match at Borussia Park and to sample the considerable delights of the bars in the cobbled streets of Mönchengladbach's Old Town. Mönchengladbach is what is known as a proper football city. The locals understand the game and they are a friendly lot who are only too happy to share their thoughts with English visitors.

Relations were first formed between Borussia Mönchengladbach and Liverpool in the 1970s when they were both among the top sides in Europe. They met in two European finals and a semi-final and Liverpool won all three so it is generous of the Germans to be so welcoming. Back then, Borussia were enjoying a glorious period in their proud history under the leadership of Hennes Weisweiler or "our Shankly" as he was described to me by the Germans.

Back to April 2010 and Borussia are safe, the sun is shining and there is a feel good, end of season mood about today's match against Bayern Munich which finishes 1-1. In a warning of what was to follow in the World Cup several weeks later, German international Miroslav Klose equalises for the visitors.

The Liverpool fans are also happy to chat with the Bayern supporters, especially as their side eliminated

Manchester United from the Champions League a week or so before our visit. One of the visiting Bavarians is wearing comedy lederhosen and happily poses for pictures with the Liverpool supporters. We are then whisked off to the inner sanctum of the 50,000-capacity ground and on to the pitch in front of the Curva Nord which is a big standing area. Flags are paraded, 'You'll Never Walk Alone is sung' and applause is returned in a show of mutual appreciation and respect between English and German fans. Afterwards, many of the Liverpool fans are still buzzing with the excitement. And no, it wasn't the alt bier.

It is fair to say that the 90 minutes that followed were not the most stirring ever seen in the Bundesliga, but despite the sedate pace of the match it was enjoyable and Reus' goal brought the ground to life. After the match, fans headed back to the Fanhaus which at first glance looks like a marquee but on closer inspection reveals itself as a former army barracks which has been converted into an impressive bar with a beer garden at the side. Inside and out the party is in full swing with more hearty renditions of 'You'll Never Walk Alone' and the Borussia theme 'Elf vom Niederrhein'. Everywhere you go there are friendly Mönchengladbach fans, many of them clad in Liverpool shirts, who are keen to tell you how good it is to see the Merseyside ambassadors in town.

In the 1970s Borussia Mönchengladbach were a big name in more ways than one in European football and a mutual respect emerged between the Germans and Liverpool. Our first European Cup final in Rome in 1977 was a watershed event for Scousers and it was also a big deal for Borussia who were looking to avenge their defeat against us in the UEFA Cup final four years earlier.

With British troops stationed in the area there had long been close links anyway and they were cemented in and around the Olympic Stadium in Rome. "We couldn't believe what we saw," one German veteran of the 1977 final told me. "Liverpool had more fans than us and out sung us but the friendship between the two clubs goes back to that match."

That friendship was further strengthened after the Hillsborough disaster when Borussia Mönchengladbach fans raised money and showed a solidarity with people on Merseyside that hasn't been forgotten. Several months before the Liverpool fans went to Germany in April 2010, a group of Borussia fans were on Merseyside for the Boxing Day win against Wolves. One of the main points made by the Borussia fans was how quiet the Kop was that day compared to how it had been in previous seasons. Remarkably, many of the Germans missed Christmas at home to travel to Liverpool and we also found out that despite the timing of the trip, demand for tickets outstripped supply.

For football fans in their forties and older, Borussia Mönchengladbach will always be a famous name in European football and the more you learn about their triumphs against the odds, the more you warm to them. Borussia transformed themselves from provincial also-rans to international powerhouse under Weisweiler's leadership. It was all the sweeter for Borussia that they were able to compete or better Bayern Munich's achievements, on the domestic stage at least. Bayern remain a truly giant club but for a time they were the undisputed giants of the continent. They monopolised the European Cup, winning it three years in a row from 1974 to 1976. Bayern had the money, the prestige and became known as FC Hollywood, but their dominance was challenged by a Borussia team which included stars such as Rainer Bonhof, Gunter Netzer, Berti Vogts and Allan Simonsen. "Die Fohlen", or "the Foals" as they are affectionately known, enjoyed a golden decade in the Seventies, winning five Bundesliga titles, including three in a row. They were still a big European force at the turn of the decade, capturing the UEFA Cup in 1979 and reaching the final 12 months later.

In the 1980s they lost most of their star names but offered a launch pad to greatness for Lothar Matthäus who spent five years at the club before hitting the big time with Bayern and Germany. The 1990s proved to be a cruel decade with a German Cup win being overshadowed by financial troubles and relegation. Staying in the Bundesliga has remained a struggle, but Borussia showed a vision of strategic planning sadly lacking at Anfield by completing a 54,000-capacity stadium for 85 million Euros and Borussia Park has now replaced the atmospheric Bokelberg as the club's home.

In 2010, the Borussia Mönchengladbach fans were following Liverpool's struggles with financial problems off the pitch and underachievement on it with a mix of interest and concern. A young supporter, Sebastian Lark, whose father is English and who follows 'Gladbach home and away, was good enough to spend an enjoyable hour over a beer explaining to me the priorities of the average German football director and administrator. They are clearly on a different planet to those of the characters who brought free market chaos of the English Premier League. The German game is more closely regulated with stricter rules on club ownership. Fans such as those at Mönchengladbach have genuine influence within their club. Yes, we want success, Lark said, but only by spending transfer money and money for wages that can be afforded. Owners piling debt on the club and failing to turn up for home matches would simply not be tolerated.

But despite the unsavoury features of modern English football ownership and Liverpool's habit of beating their beloved club in the 1970s, the Kop is almost a holy place to the German fans. Merseysider Graham Agg who, as we shall see has played a key role in the development of friendly relations between Borussia and Liverpool, said: "Anfield to the Germans is like a mythical stadium. I get many emails from Germans saying 'before I die I want to go to Anfield.'"

Agg, who is in the German Reds which is an affiliated official supporters club, is the Liverpool fan who has done most to promote goodwill with the Mönchengladbach fans. From his home in Netherton, he is a tireless organiser, sending out emails, booking hotel rooms and sorting out match tickets for the two friendship weekends. His powers of persuasion are well known on the Kop where fans sitting near him are regularly persuaded to go to Germany for the first time or make a return booking. Agg firmly believes that the ancient tabloid football prejudices and tensions between England and Germany have nothing to do with him or Liverpool supporters. He spent 10 years working in engineering all over the country and found much in common with German people. By 2006, he was on the committee of the German Reds and already knew that Borussia fans travelled to Liverpool each season to take in a game so as a fluent German speaker, it was natural he would catch up with the travelling supporters in Liverpool city centre.

"We had a great night and right at the end, in January 2006, one of the Mönchengladbach fans said to me 'This friendship between Liverpool and us is fantastic but the only thing is it is one-sided. We have been coming here every year since 1992 and apart from a couple of visitors from Liverpool nothing official has been done.' I was quite embarrassed as a Liverpudlian, born and bred here. I thought 'it's totally wrong that we haven't reciprocated this visit'.

"So I organised a visit to coincide with the 30th anniversary of the European Cup final, 1977. That was supposed to be a one-off. It wasn't planned to make it an annual friendship visit. But because of the way we were greeted and the way we were treated it was unbelievable. We were treated like royalty. I decided that we would have to make this an annual trip."

From an initial cohort of 30, the numbers travelling to Mönchengladbach have grown each year and there were 71 in April 2010. Not bad, considering airspace was closed in the days leading up to the Liverpool fans' visit because of the volcanic ash clouds. Newbies such as me on the Mönchengladbach trip were told to expect a warm welcome and we weren't disappointed. Agg calls the reception given to Liverpool fans "mind blowing".

"To put it into context, if you walk around the centre of Mönchengladbach with a Liverpool top on you will be stopped by the locals who want to buy you a drink and talk football with you," Agg says. "Liverpool are by far the most popular English club in Mönchengladbach – and I would say Germany as well – because of our history, even more so than Manchester United. It is because of our clashes with Mönchengladbach in the seventies, Hamburg and Borussia Dortmund going back to the 60s, and Bayern Munich."

Agg and the regulars on the Mönchengladbach trip are rightfully proud that there is now a genuine exchange of fans between the two clubs and media interest is building with growing radio, newspaper and online coverage about the friendship in both countries.

"It is gradually getting bigger and bigger," says Agg. "A lot of people know about it now because it is publicised on the website and it has been recognised by Liverpool FC. Brian Hall, the PR manager, always sends me something to present to 'Gladbach's officials. When I look back now if that fan had not said to me what he said it probably would never have happened. I thought 'we should do something here.'

"Also when you go over you are ambassadors for the city and Liverpool FC; it is a great thing to do. This tradition of taking a friendship flag which they allow us to unveil on the pitch is amazing. The second year we went in 2008 – their president and vice president came on to the pitch to greet us. It was amazing he did that. We have the backing of both clubs, it's great. A mate of mine, Gary Johnson, has been to all seven European Cup finals. He was on the pitch when the Borussia Mönchengladbach fans were singing 'You'll Never Walk Alone' and he broke into tears. He said, 'I have been all over the world watching Liverpool and this weekend has been even better than going to a European Cup final because of the way we have been treated.' I thought when he said that it made it all worthwhile. It took a lot of organisation and took a lot of my time up. But when someone like that, a Liverpool fan through and through, says that it makes you realise what sort of weekend it was."

Football has a lot wrong with it, but when you see the common respect between fans from Mönchengladbach and Merseyside you can't help but feel good that this old game can still bring people together like nothing else.

6.

For love, not money

"Clubs need to come down from planet football and live in the real world." **Grant Bather, Virgin Money**

Do you fancy watching Liverpool home and away, not missing a match all season? For most of us cost and opportunity prevent us from being ever present fans. But what about the most dedicated who go everywhere? In the 2009-10 season, I calculated how much it would cost as a minimum to see every minute of the Reds' first team matches in person. Before I reveal the total, it is instructive to note that these sums didn't include 40 different types of costs associated with being a football fan – only match travel and admission prices were considered. After much tapping on a calculator I worked out that the most dedicated fans of all spent between £3,771 and £4,164. Minimum. In 2009-10 season there was a wide range of prices and there were discounts for OAPs, younger fans etc for certain matches, so the costs I state are based on an adult paying full whack.

Now for some background. Total match admission was £1,720, which is almost exactly the same as the cost of European travel to seven matches in the Champions League and Europa Cup. Incidentally, globetrotters attending all those matches would have totted up more than 12,000 miles following their passion. The figures stated above assume that the fan lives very near to Anfield and so doesn't incur costs for travel to home matches. They also assume that the fan is a season ticket holder whose match costs over a season average out at £34 per home game. The £3,771 figure is based on the cost of travel to away matches by coach and the higher total relates to going to matches by car (buying petrol at the most competitive prices and driving a relatively economical vehicle). A Liverpool supporter driving to all home matches from the South East could expect to pay an extra £1,000 or so on top of the £4k although he or she would, of course, save money on away travel for London matches.

The lowest recorded admission price I found was £7.50 to watch the Unirea away match in the Europa League and the highest ticket prices were £51 which gave some the chance to watch the defeats at White Hart Lane and Old Trafford. Now remember, no one does anything anywhere without paying for food, drink, parking, etc. Also remember that the figures take no account of a potential cost of £300-£400 for TV subscriptions to Sky, ESPN etc.

It is impossible ever to say whether football offers value for money, but let's assume that few fans enjoyed a season that contained 19 defeats in all competitions with the only real highlight being Liverpool's appearance in the last four of a second rate European competition. But the fan who never misses a match would have spent the equivalent of £14 to see each home league goal and other ways, I would suggest that they spent much more in the bars of Lisbon, Madrid and Budapest anyway.

It all adds up to a frightening bill for the most devoted. In many cases following Liverpool to this extent will take up all of a fan's disposable income and we also have to factor in a further cost – that of previous attendance. Tickets for away matches are allocated on a loyalty basis and in 2009-10 the typical away allocation for league matches involving Liverpool was around 2,500. To be one of this number, your fan card, which has details of previous matches attended, would need to show that you had been to a certain number of away matches the season before which might range from one to 15. In a nutshell, to have the chance to spend a fortune following Liverpool in 2009-10 you needed to demonstrate that you had already emptied your bank account doing the same thing the previous campaign. Liverpool FC moved to a loyalty based system for allocating tickets around 2003. Previously, the right to buy a ticket for high demand away matches was based on a season ticket holder's serial number. *The Kop* newspaper lobbied successfully for a move to fans being rewarded for showing the most commitment. But in the summer of 2010, *The Kop* was reporting that changes were being considered which would enable a wider range of fans to have access to tickets in the away sections of Liverpool matches. It is proving impossible to keep everyone happy and, to make matters worse for fans, the UK economy was in deep trouble when this book was published. Fans from all Premier League clubs have felt the pinch in recent years. There is every sign that more fans will find it difficult to attend matches in an era of wage freezes, redundancies and job insecurity. The

Premier League has squeezed every penny out of the fans with a deliberate and cynical policy of hyping up run of the mill matches as "events" that supporters from all across the world would happily bankrupt themselves to be a part of. In 2010 I spent £7 for a standing ticket at Shakespeare's Globe Theatre in London and almost £40 to sit at Anfield. If you had told me these figures in the late 1980s I would have been convinced that you had got the previous sentence the wrong way round.

Rising ticket costs have meant that many fans simply cannot afford to go to the game. In the 1980s, Liverpool suffered huge unemployment and gates were hit, even when we were winning league titles season after season. But you knew then that the Kop with its standing and pay on the gate admission was still just about accessible for those on low or no wages. In the early 1970s, a fan taking home about £15 a week forked out a mere 40p to stand on the terraces at Anfield and in 1988-89 when I was a student, my Kop season ticket was £57, a sum that would barely cover two discounted European or League Cup matches these days. Getting access to match tickets (or more accurately getting your fan card "activated") can often depend on fans having credit or debit cards and access to the Liverpoolfc.tv website. What happens then if you can't get online, aren't able to afford to hang on the telephone to speak to an operator or prefer to deal in cash? The answer is: you don't get in until the rare day when there isn't much demand for a match and you can pay on the gate just like you used to.

The national picture shows that the price hike in tickets has been relentless from the inception of the Premier League until the 2010-11 season. A Football Task Force survey estimated that in 1988 average season ticket prices across all four English divisions was £73. If season ticket prices had kept pace with inflation, by 2004 the average English Football League season ticket price would have been £123, instead of the average of £325 it was found to be in a follow up study that year.

In 2007, the *Independent on Sunday* put into sharp focus an issue which cropped up many times in my discussions with Reds. The paper interviewed a plasterer, Dan, who lived in Anfield.

> "Supporters love their clubs intensely, irrationally, and at great expense," The IOS reported. "Jamie, 10, lives within walking distance of Anfield. He sleeps under a Liverpool duvet that cost £30 and wears a full replica strip that was £50, but has only seen the team once. "My granddad took me a lot when I was a kid," says his father Dan, "but I can't do that for the lad."

This touches a nerve with Les Lawson, secretary of the Merseyside Supporters' Branch. Lawson is of a generation bitten by the football bug when life was simpler and admission costs were within reach of working class fans. He still never misses a home game, but when he looks around the ground on match days he sees an ageing fan base and an absence of young, local supporters. Lawson believes imaginative ways must be found to provide affordable seats for younger Reds.

Lawson said: "In my example I first went to the game in the late 1960s, early 1970s with my dad. I started playing football and when I realised I wasn't good enough to play at a higher level I decided I wanted to watch Liverpool every week (this was in the 1976-77 season). Then you could pay to get on the Kop so my habit was started in 1976 and, touch wood, I haven't missed a home game since in any competition, including friendlies and testimonials. I was able to get into the habit of going to the game at 13, 14. But what worries me as a football supporter in my mid-forties is you see a lot of kids in the street wearing Liverpool shirts, but how many of them go to the games? How many of them wear shirts because they are brought up that way by the parents or because all the kids in school get the new Liverpool kit? That support is vital for 10, 20 years' time. There is nowhere for a group of mates in school to decide to go to the game the next day as we used to. You used to have to queue up at 1pm or earlier if it was a big game, but you used to do it and it was all part of learning to be a Liverpool supporter, a football supporter.

"There is going to be a generation who is not aware of how to support the club. The average age for a supporter now is between 40 and 45 and you wonder where the support is going to come from in 20 years. I am lucky, I have had a season ticket for 25-30 years but the other thing that has gone is the spontaneity, the chat of going to the game, of inviting people you haven't seen for a while to go with you. That can't happen now. If the new stadium ever gets off the ground it is something the club do have to look at seriously because it isn't just about today. It is fine getting 40-odd thousand every game, but the problem is now that if when I was 13, 14 and I had to get a dad and lad ticket to go to the game I might not have been able to get to nearly a quarter of the games I went to. And if I hadn't been to those games, would I still be going now and would I still be as passionate?"

At the start of the 2009-10 season, Virgin Money published a series of revealing press releases which showed that fans were struggling to meet the financial demands of following Premier League football. Despite the economic austerity, Virgin showed that the Football Inflation Index, which examines the cost of items such as petrol, match tickets, food, alcohol and replica shirts, had risen by 14%.

In other words football's greed was out of step with the people who had fuelled its dramatic upsurge in popularity for 15 years or more. And while Liverpool, Manchester United and others ran up debts as a result of "leveraged buy-outs" fans were going into debt just to carry on going to the match. Virgin's research showed that 21% of Liverpool fans surveyed were in debt as a result of following their team – through "football related borrowings" – which amounted to an average of £1,155 per supporter. The fears of Les Lawson and others were supported by a Virgin Money statistic that showed only 17% of Liverpool fans can afford to take their children to games while 28% struggle to do so. "Clubs need to come down from planet football and live in the real world," Grant Bather a spokesperson for Virgin Money said.

For some, the unequal struggle to support a Liverpool FC habit has already been lost. A group of dedicated Liverpool supporters formed their own non-League team, AFC Liverpool, to enable Reds who can't afford to go to Anfield to enjoy at least some of the experience of a match day at a fraction of the cost. The AFC Liverpool story is featured elsewhere in this book, but co-founder Alun Parry freely admits that money was a driving force in the establishment of a new grass roots club.

He said: "If there was a political issue for me it was the idea that football was eating itself to such an extent that the whole integrity of the competition was up for sale. It was about affordability. The average age of a football fan now in the Premiership is 43. It is about those Reds who watch the game in pubs and can't take their kids to Anfield. I support Liverpool Football Club, not the business. If you look at AFC Wimbledon they have had their club taken off them, but in the same way people who used to be able to go to the game and can't, have had their club taken off them. I used to go to the game every week with my dad and my brother, but his kids can't. In fact he takes them to Anfield to savour the atmosphere and watches the game in a pub."

On the eve of the 2010-11 season, there was a reminder that someone somewhere needs to pay for the spiralling costs of players wages and leveraged buy-outs. As usual, that someone is you and me. It was a case of good news, bad news on July 20, 2010 when Joe Cole's move from Chelsea and Steven Gerrard's decision to stay at Anfield were announced at the same time as the club told us that match day costs were going up by up to 15% for the most popular fixtures. Season ticket holders had previously been told they would need to spend seven per cent more for home matches in 2010-11. Forty pounds a match has always felt like a very high price to pay at Anfield. Costs have almost doubled in just over a decade. No wonder the Premier League has regularly been called the Greed-is-Good League by veteran journalist Brian Glanville.

Of course some will find the money no matter what. Chris Le Neve attended all of Liverpool's seven European Cup finals and, like many fans at the time, he made a big sacrifice to attend the first of those games in Rome 1977. "My Tamla Motown collection was my pride and joy, but I was out of work at the time and I needed to get the money to go to Italy. So I sold the records for £100 which covered the cost of the coach travel and ticket. On the way back the coach was impounded about 200 miles from Paris and we had to get the British Embassy to help us get home." Nowadays he has "indoctrinated" his wife Karen, who wasn't previously a football supporter. The couple are dedicated fans and travel home and away from their home in Scunthorpe where Chris is secretary of the LFC supporters' branch.

"We don't even want to calculate how much supporting Liverpool costs us," Chris admits and Karen adds: "Now we plan our holidays around Liverpool matches. They are expensive trips and we have raised money through car boot sales. I don't think now there will ever be a time when we are not going to watch Liverpool play football."

In the late 1960s, Arthur Hopcraft wrote an influential book called *The Football Man* which looked at the game through the eyes of players, directors, referees, journalists and fans. Some of Hopcraft's observations on match costs make interesting reading more than 40 years on, although we must remember that since his book was first published, inflation and decimalisation have made it difficult to compare costs then and now in Britain. But in 1968 an average fan might earn £22 a week and Hopcroft said that this "enabled him to see all the football he wanted and also to go away for an annual holiday". Hopcroft referred to a Manchester City fan who could follow his team to

Merseyside or Yorkshire for less than £1 (ticket and transport). London aways cost more than £3 and the City fan and his mates watched the pennies or "went carefully on food and drink".

Hopcroft added: "The football fan is not just a watcher. His sweat and his nerves work on football, and his spirit can be made rich or destitute by it."

Well travelled Liverpool fans can well relate to this many years later. The destitute bit in particular.

7.

'Them Scousers Again'

"There is something about being a Scouser that is different from being from London and elsewhere. We like that honesty, the humour and the history of the club." **Guy Prowse, South African Liverpool supporter**

If you want some idea of the importance of football on Merseyside, there are plenty of examples. The huge crowds which lined the streets to celebrate Liverpool's trophy successes in 2005 and 2006 are a good start. But my favourite emerged before the 2010 General Election in Britain. An ambitious, young Labour candidate from the south of England, Luciana Berger, was named prospective parliamentary candidate for the Liverpool Wavertree seat which is Fort Knox safe. Berger was duly elected but not before what could have been a damaging "gaffe". The *Liverpool Echo* reported: "Her lack of local knowledge was exposed when she could not say who Anfield legend Bill Shankly was or who sang 'Ferry Across the Mersey'."

That may tell us you wouldn't want Luciana in your team on a pub quiz night, and it might also show that she had a lot of homework to do to find out more about a city that has history, legends and heroes in its DNA. It also tells you – and Luciana will now be fully aware of this –Liverpool isn't like anywhere else.

It should go without saying that Liverpool is a club of the city. The ground is located two or three miles north of the city centre in a working class area and the football team has always been central to life on Merseyside – as long as you don't support Everton. But in recent years, Liverpool's support has changed. Rising ticket prices and surging demand for big games have led to growing numbers of football tourists or more casual supporters watching matches at Anfield. Add to that the growth in numbers of fans joining affiliated supporters' branches around the UK and the world, and the trend in the 1970s and 1980s for lots of people to leave the city and you have many fans following Liverpool who don't live there. It seems that overall the Scouse to non-Scouse support is about 50/50 on match days, although in certain parts of the ground the ratio shifts considerably.

Les Lawson, secretary of the Merseyside branch of the Supporters' Association, knows all about the special dedication shown by fans closest to home. Lawson highlights the quality of the support as much as the depth, which makes Liverpool FC a special case. He said: "Some fans go abroad and won't miss a match, they have been to Vladikavkaz and everywhere following the Reds and they deserve all the praise in the world for the support they show and the level of commitment in the pocket. That is what you call loyalty and that is what the club means to the supporters. Every club has supporters who won't miss a game, but I do think that Liverpool supporters are by far the best in world football for the level of support and they are very knowledgeable. They know when the support is really needed they will get right behind the team and go to that extra level. That's where the term "12th Man" comes from and it is fully deserved."

That "12th Man" tag has now been claimed by LFC as part of its merchandising strategy, but it was also used as a tribute to the late Bobby Wilcox who was described as a Liverpool FC super fan. A prominent figure in local league football, Wilcox died aged 60 in January 2009. Jamie Carragher and Phil Thompson led the tributes and journalist Tony Barrett – then with the *Echo* and now with *The Times* – wrote: "His service to his club was unstinting and it was unconditional. It was also so dedicated that it set him apart in the eyes of so many of Liverpool's fan base as someone to be looked up to and whose lead should be followed."

Barrett reported that at Wilcox's funeral, the Shankly Gates were opened to allow his procession around Anfield and the flags were lowered to half mast. Everyone from the board room, the ticket office, the stands, the pub and the local playing field had a tale and a fond memory of Wilcox. These stories featured in an *LFC TV* special and one of the floral tributes was for "Bobby, the ticket master".

"If you needed a ticket, you rang Bobby and if he couldn't get you one, Rafa couldn't," one of his many friends said on the programme.

From all accounts Wilcox symbolised some old fashioned Anfield qualities of sportsmanship and support for his club, no matter what. Unwritten laws of match day attendance include backing the team from first minute to last and always clapping the visiting keeper when he runs towards the Kop goal. One of Bill Shankly's many legacies has been to encourage partisan support for Liverpool with an understanding that it takes two to make a match and to respect the opposition, even in the heat of battle. But most of all, Shankly suggested unity and 100 per cent commitment to the cause were non-negotiable qualities. Many Liverpool fans don't run Liverpool down whatever the circumstances.

Wilcox's friends say he would never criticise Liverpool publicly and this is something which many match goers would understand. For many, whingeing on *Radio Five Live* or on online message boards is just not the done thing. Scousers might take a different view when they contact Radio Merseyside or City FM, but somehow that isn't as destructive as sharing criticism with a national audience. "Keeping matters in house" was a long established principle which has been tested more and more in recent years. Usually, a poor result at Anfield is greeted by a collective groan of disappointment, but little else. It says something about the loyalty of the fans that booing is a news story in its own right. Consider the reaction to Liverpool's goalless draw with West Ham in the 2008-09 season. There were many grumbles on the final whistle, but the catcalls from a sizeable minority in Anfield – on a night when we went back to the top of the league – attracted much comment. It wasn't what you expected at Liverpool. Interviewed on the *LFC TV* programme, the pop singer, writer and Liverpool fan Peter Hooton suggested the Bobby Wilcox generation represented the old style of Anfield support – wholehearted, patient and knowledgeable. There is an implication that younger fans are influenced by the demand for instant success and are seduced by a media too quick to shout "tell us what you think".

Experienced former managers such as Graham Taylor and David Pleat, who have no connections with Merseyside, have both remarked on *BBC Five Live* that Liverpool fans have a genuine understanding and feel for the game that is more noticeable there than in other places. The journalist Charles Lambert has been covering matches on Merseyside since the early 1970s and reckons fans at Anfield demonstrate a number of qualities that make them something more than the average Premier League spectator.

"The thing about Liverpool fans is they are always so articulate," said Lambert. "They always have very well thought out views. Obviously they don't agree with people all the time and it means that whenever you talk to them you know you are going to get interesting material. They know their stuff and they can put it across well, often with a dash of humour which makes it worth listening to. That was always quite rewarding. It is a cliché to say that Liverpool fans are more passionate and more knowledgeable and more humorous that supporters elsewhere and it is easy to fall into the trap of saying 'yeah, yeah they are'. I actually think that what makes them unique is the combination of those things. I have been to Celtic and I have never seen a more passionate set of fans, ever. I think they are at least as passionate as Liverpool's, if not more. You can go to Newcastle or Glasgow and the supporters are just as knowledgeable there as they are at Liverpool and Everton. Manchester City fans have a great sense of humour. But it is the combination of all of those things that makes the Merseyside supporter unique in my experience."

One of the traditional ways of sharing these views is the local radio phone-in. Each Monday during the season at 7pm on a Monday night *BBC Radio Merseyside's* Alan Jackson takes calls from Reds and Blues. In the studio there is always an Evertonian and a Liverpool supporter. To ignore this requirement would be like a politics programme failing to balance government and opposition ministers in a debate. Even in these two hours you hear a better informed standard of comment from the fans than you would on national stations. Zonal marking, box to box midfielders, filling the boxes, protecting full backs and the minutiae of Steven Gerrard's role in the team, mood, etc are picked apart in great detail. Holding it all together, Jackson plays devil's advocate, a classic tactic of the talk show host. If someone criticises the American owners' transfer policy, he will defend it or at least attempt to make some sense of it. If someone slags off Ryan Babel, he will argue that the Dutchman is playing out of position.

The local radio phone-in is a fascinating exercise in eavesdropping. It's a slice of soccer life in a football mad city. One minute there is a discussion of the merits of Lucas Leiva and the next a caller from Maghull wants to talk about Bob Paisley, the standard of the pies or the pillars in the Main Stand. Callers and listeners to Radio Merseyside are more likely to be older fans who can remember Liverpool's most successful days. In fact many of them were going to the match when we were in the old, old Second Division.

A tricky debate was opened up on Radio Merseyside during the 2009-10 season by Jake from Dingle who said he was fed up with the lack of match day atmosphere and the fact that "you never sit next to someone from

Liverpool in the ground. If there were 45,000 Scousers in the ground then the place would be rocking."

But following Liverpool was never just about coming from the city, even though the Scousers have always been the most passionate. Fans from out of town have always followed the club and surely it is ridiculous for anyone to complain about people from Northern Ireland or the Republic travelling to matches at Anfield. If it wasn't for Ireland and its 19th Century immigrants, there wouldn't be a city of Liverpool at all. But since the formation of the Premier League and Liverpool's 2005 Champions League win, new generations of supporters with no obvious family connections to Merseyside have become more common at Anfield. An Evertonian's banner said "Welcome to Merseyside, Liverpool fans" in a dig at the out of town followers a couple of years ago. The issue attracts significant correspondence in the monthly *Kop* newspaper which is careful to differentiate between genuine fans and "day trippers" or "tourists" whose authenticity is open to question.

Graham Agg, who comes from Netherton, and is a season ticket holder at Anfield, believes the out of towner debate is really a non-issue. "As far as I am concerned if you are a Liverpool fan, you are a Liverpool fan and it doesn't matter where you come from, London, Scotland, Ireland, Norway, Germany. I think it is something we should be proud of. I embrace it totally. When an Evertonian says to me 'you have fans from Norway, Ireland, Germany' I say 'yeah, you're right.' They don't know where to go then. Because I don't go on the defensive – we have fans all over the world. Everton haven't. That is all down to our history. I think the 'out-of-towners' thing usually crops up when people talk about lack of atmosphere at Anfield. The out-of-towners get the blame then. But I am totally against that. We should be proud that people are happy to pay a lot of money and take a flight to Liverpool to watch us."

Like Agg, the magazine editor and blogger Gareth Roberts, believes you don't need a Liverpool postcode to follow the team, although he is uneasy that some fans seem able to disconnect themselves from the city where they watch their football. In the 1980s the opposite was true with out of town Liverpool supporters immersing themselves in the local music and club scene. Some even adopted the accent.

But Roberts said: "I witnessed one incident in particular which I found amazing. People were taking pictures of derelict houses around Anfield and laughing about it, basically saying, 'what a shithole'. I just didn't understand the logic. You are supporting Liverpool Football Club and yet you are knocking Liverpool. It is one and the same thing. This is a football club of the city. How can you mock the city and support the club? This does go on with the out of town support. They are not all like that by any means. A lot do take the whole thing to heart which is fine, which is good. But some supporters you see at Anfield seem to be almost there for the experience, to tick it off and say 'we have been to Anfield'.

"You see a lot them not actually watching the game. They are taking pictures, videos. Texting their mates to say they are there and taping it on their mobile when everyone is singing 'You'll Never Walk Alone.' It's as if they want to go back to wherever they are from and say 'look, look I went to Anfield' and paste it up on Facebook or wherever. They don't seem to have any real interest in the team. I was in the Kop once and it was a bad game, to be fair. We lost and it was a poor performance. There was a person sitting by me who wasn't from the city. He actually stood up about 70 minutes in, got up and walked out. His words were 'I am fed up with this Scouse shit'. I don't understand this. Things like that do puzzle me."

Local Liverpool supporters are wary of 'whoppers' who are best described as fans who attach themselves to the team but have little awareness of match day support and the traditions of following the club. As we will see in the chapter on atmosphere, supporting the club sometimes feels like breaking the code of a secret society and credibility is significant to many fans at Anfield who are determined not to be like everyone else at other clubs. You won't hear the Kop singing "Liverpool till I die" any time soon.

But the debate is far more complicated than being a simple case of out of town fans not "getting" Liverpool. In fact, in Anil Patel, who helps run the Hertfordshire supporters' branch, believes that more should be done to attract more young Merseysiders into Anfield for matches. He is a genuine champion of the city, its culture as well as its football. "Scousers are welcoming and I don't believe they mind supporters who follow Liverpool from outside the city," he said. "However, they (non-Scousers) should keep to the tradition of the club and respect the people and city of Liverpool. I once heard 'it's not the accent that's important but the attitude' and I totally agree with this. I love Liverpool as much as anyone even though I don't come from there. I take my son there in the summer and show him the city. If anyone says anything against Liverpool we will always defend the city and the people as well. The reason I have continued to go to every Liverpool home game for 20 years is because of the way the fans follow this club and the traditions. If I supported any other club I wouldn't have as much commitment to that team as I do for Liverpool. We don't want any Mickey-taking about Scousers robbing stuff and mimicking their voices and so on. If they (branch members) support Liverpool they should appreciate the city and its people. We are guests there and we should be privileged to support the club and be honoured that the people of Liverpool allow us to support that club with no problems."

Another "Scouserphile" is Anders Gustavsson who did a university thesis from Oslo University on Liverpool supporters' attitudes and has supported the club since the 1980s. "A lot of Norwegians like the pubs in Liverpool and also when you get to know people from Liverpool they are very friendly," he said. "They have a good sense of humour but it takes a little time to understand it as they are very direct. There are a lot of Norwegians going to Liverpool to study at LIPA (Liverpool Institute of Performing Arts). It is football, music and the people that appeal. The city centre is small and easy to get around."

South African Liverpool fan Riccardo Jansen fulfilled a long-time ambition in 2006 when he visited Liverpool for the first time. Many have compared following Liverpool with religious worship and for Jansen it really was a pilgrimage. He said: "Only two of us in our branch have been to Anfield. I stayed in Wavertree for four weeks on holiday. It was a good feeling. I stayed with an Evertonian who is 75 and he took me around Liverpool. I went to Mathew Street, saw where the Beatles started and I saw the Mersey which was great and I enjoyed travelling around by bus. I went to the Benfica Champions League game and then I went to watch Liverpool v Charlton. For the Champions League game I was on the Kop and that was massive experience for me. It was like heaven and I didn't want to come home. I felt this is the place I want to live. Hopefully one day, if I have an opportunity I will definitely live over there. The way the Liverpudlians made me feel was great and I could not have asked for anything better. They were very open with me and made me feel at home."

Elsewhere in South Africa, Guy Prowse, a Liverpool fan since 1974, reckons the combination of the FA Cup final win that year and the fact his mate from school was originally from Birkenhead – a short ferry ride away from Liverpool – helped him become a supporter for life. "There is a lot in Scouse culture, a lot of the ethos that you associate with Liverpool with working class people who don't always have things their own way and it seems your back is up against the wall. There is a lot of empathy in South Africa for that type of situation. There is an honesty about the city that appeals to a lot of South Africans. There is something about being a Scouser that is different from being from London and elsewhere. We like that honesty, the humour and the history of the club."

Prowse is one of many Liverpool supporters around the world who believe the club's unique appeal is largely due to its traditions, but no doubt he would understand the plight of Neil Rodgers, from Huyton, who believes we live in more cynical, money-centred times. Unfortunately, like many fans, he is no longer able to attend as many games as he would like. He said: "In the

70s, 80s and 90s I got to as many games as I could but in 2009-10 I was unable to get tickets for the games and the season before I went to about six games. Liverpool FC have forgotten the Liverpool people who stood on the Kop back in the 1960s who built the club up to where it is today. Today Liverpool FC are a business and in my opinion, many Liverpool fans would sell a ticket to someone who lives outside of the L postcode area before selling it to someone who has a Liverpool postcode. A family of four from Devon will probably spend the weekend in Liverpool, spend money in the Liverpool FC shop, buy a programme, food and drink. It's all money for Liverpool FC."

Some are born to Scouseness and some have Scouseness thrust upon them. Les McKee is one such case. A native of Northern Ireland, he loved the city so much he gave up his home and job and moved to Liverpool. He had to sleep on friends' floors before getting fixed up with work and moving to the suburb of Aigburth. His devotion led to him being named Merseyside Sports Fan of the Year by the local media in 2008. "Every day is amazing and I am living the life I dreamt of as a kid. Liverpool is my home now and I class myself as Scouse," he told the *Liverpool Echo*.

Recent events at Liverpool FC have warned us not to take much for granted, but there is an umbilical cord between Merseyside and its football that is unlikely ever to be broken. Scousers, out-of- towners and even Labour MPs soon figure that out.

Rivals in blue – and red

*"**Liverpool** is as synonymous with sport as it is with music. From Premiership football to top-class rugby league and the spellbinding excitement of the Grand National, the region is renowned for its sporting success."*
Manchester Evening News (two days after Istanbul!)

The Merseytravel bus was about to turn right when it stopped at traffic lights near Liverpool's Royal University Hospital before heading into town. Most of the passengers had seen Liverpool beat Burnley 4-0 at Anfield an hour before and there was a quiet satisfaction of three points gained. The bus was about to set off when a teenager of about 13 or 14 briefly glanced towards the crowded lower deck. He wasn't angry and seemed to act out of instinctive tribal loyalty when he shouted "Kopites are gobshites". Everyone on the bus heard it, no one was surprised and some even found it funny. And with that our young Evertonian went on his way, walking towards Kensington Fields, cheered by a harmless bit of Red baiting.

In Newcastle or Leeds, the clubs are the only football show in town, but in Liverpool Red and Blue have had to co-exist over many years. Liverpool's birth in 1892 was the result of a boardroom fall out at Everton Football Club and the relationship between the two sides from across Stanley Park has been a cause of fascination ever since. Rivalry between Liverpool and Everton is tribal and it also cuts across families. Two quick examples from my own experience. By rights, my dad should have been an Evertonian given family loyalty but he followed Liverpool instead, in contrast to his younger brother. Several years ago one of my colleagues was a Liverpool fan who was married to a very keen Evertonian who insisted his two sons be loyal to Glawdys Street and not the Kop. There are countless other cases of families, friends and neighbours being divided by football.

More than thirty years ago, I found out just how painful it could be to lose to Everton. In 1978, the Blues had just beaten Liverpool 1-0 on a sunny Saturday afternoon at Goodison Park. Andy King scored the only goal in front of the Liverpool supporters at the Park End. It was the first time in seven years that Liverpool had lost to their nearest rivals, and the image of King with arms aloft remains burnt into my mind like a bad migraine. Straight after the game a BBC journalist attempted to interview King on the pitch only to be ordered on to the touchline in no uncertain terms by a police officer who might also have been a Liverpool supporter given his expression. I walked down Queen's Drive on my way home to West Derby with my dad after watching the match. I knew we were in for a verbal onslaught. In those days I still wore a scarf and seeing this, the Blues were encouraged to tell us what they thought of

Liverpool. I was only 12 at the time and I could not remember the previous Everton win against us. After running the gauntlet on a walk that seemed to take forever, we and our fellow Reds went home to grumble about the result and remark how "all these Evertonians have come out of the woodwork". At school on Monday, more Blues wanted to discuss the match with us. We took our medicine and told them that: "OK, you've had your big win, but we'll still win the league." And we were right. But it still made it all the more important that we beat Everton next time.

My maternal granddad was a Liverpool season ticket holder who was so anti-Everton it was hilarious. He would not hear a good word said about the club, its players or anything connected to Goodison Park. Bill Shankly's quote about two great clubs in Liverpool – Liverpool and Liverpool Reserves – reminds me of my granddad to this day.

The relationship between supporters of Everton and Liverpool has been compared to an ancient family dispute with plenty of history surrounding the squabbles on both sides. Evertonians see themselves as the true team of the city. They remind Reds that their club was around before ours and they also love to trot out a quote from their late and revered hard man Brian Labone who once said: "One Evertonian is worth 10 Liverpudlians." When David Moyes took over as Everton manager he called his new employers "The People's Club". This was quickly turned into a branding exercise by EFC who sold car stickers with that logo on. It is also plastered over the outside of the Park End stand at Goodison, the same place where I was sitting when Andy King ruined my weekend all those years ago. Everton fans like to remind Liverpool supporters about the club's out of town support, but the Blues have plenty of backing outside Merseyside, albeit not as much as Liverpool. Where I now live near Chorley in Lancashire, I see more than a few Cahill shirts and North Wales has long been recognised as an Everton stronghold. There is a big London contingent of Blues and they also seem to be well followed in Stafford.

Ian Abraham, a Liverpool fan since the age of five, knows all about the background of the Liverpool/Everton dispute. But he reckons that being away from his native Merseyside has helped him become tolerant towards the Blues. It almost makes him nostalgic for the days when he could wind up Evertonians. He said: "When I came to London I found that not a lot of people liked my accent and I became even 'stauncher'. Even now I don't dislike Everton – apart from on Derby Day when I will be screaming abuse like everyone else. I see a victory for Liverpool and Everton as a victory for the city and my hatred is pure and unadulterated for Man United. I try and hate Chelsea but I just can't be bothered. I am a very proud Scouser – almost card carrying. My accent has waned but we are going back north at some point and I'll be 50 in about 14 years or so and by then it will be time to go home. I do get a little tired of the (does Harry Enfield impression) 'ay, ay, calm down.' You get browbeaten by it but there are rare days when you just think 'sod off and change the tune.'"

Liverpool, whose ground is less than a mile from Goodison, used to be Merseyside's joke team. In the 1950s Everton had the reputation, the pulling power and the wealth to lord it over the Reds. It wasn't until Bill

Shankly arrived in 1959 that the whole picture changed. Throughout the 1960s there was great rivalry between Liverpool and Everton. If 1966 is memorable at Anfield for a league title win, it is fondly remembered across the park for the Blues recovering from 2-0 down to beat Sheffield Wednesday 3-2 in an epic FA Cup final. Everton and Liverpool were drawn together in the FA Cup tie a year later. Not only did 65,000 pack into Goodison but demand for tickets was so great that eight giant screens had to be put up at Anfield where about 40,000 fans paid a total of £12,000 to see the Blues winning 1-0 with Alan Ball scoring.*

After more than a decade of obscurity, Everton were a force again in the mid to late 1980s under Howard Kendall and it was during this decade that the two Merseyside teams met three times in Wembley finals. All of them were eventually won by Liverpool, most poignantly in 1989 in the aftermath of Hillsborough. These matches were known as the "friendly finals" and much of the media coverage focused on how Red and Blue travelled to the match together in good nature. There was little need for segregation in the ground and after 1984's League Cup final both sets of fans sang "Merseyside, Merseyside" as the teams did a lap of honour together.

Two factors seemed to help that spirit of Scouse camaraderie – the fact that the match was goalless and a common cause with the enemy the shape of Margaret Thatcher, who was Prime Minister at the time. Back then, the city of Liverpool was on a collision course with the Conservative Government and the further to the right Thatcher went, the more Liverpool seemed to move the other way. At Wembley, fans from both clubs wore stickers saying "I support our council" in red and blue colours, a wise PR move by the hard left leadership running the local authority at the time.

But even then there were some who believed all the friendly derby stuff was overplayed. *The End*, a celebrated music, sport and lifestyle fanzine from the era, argued that fights were common between Red and Blue in town after Derby matches. No wonder many publicans' greatest wish was a draw whenever the two sides met. Sadly, in the 1990s the mood became bleaker and more threatening. This resulted in nasty incidents involving fans at both Anfield and Goodison. Personal abuse of players got worse and the atmosphere was often venomous. After Liverpool's 3-2 win at Anfield in 1999 – the Robbie Fowler line sniffing game – I could sense the tension in the air and it was fortunate that there weren't major problems outside the ground. There were groups of Evertonians who were clearly spoiling for a fight on that occasion.

These days, Merseyside Police have to issue appeals before Derbies for fans on both sides not to overstep the mark. Some reckon the ill feeling dates back to the mid-1980s when the Heysel ban denied Everton the chance to play in the European Cup. Others suggest the clubs have grown apart because they are businesses fighting for a similar market and the old style hands across the Park philosophy just doesn't work anymore.

Whatever the cause, it would be a shame if the healthy rivalry between Everton and Liverpool fans was ever to be lost completely. There has always been banter between the two sets of fans and when it isn't taken too seriously or when it doesn't descend into foul abuse it is still funny.

Note that when Everton were planning a ground move Liverpool fans sang: "Fuck off to Kirkby, the city's all ours" only for Evertonians to hit back with: "Fuck off to Norway, the city's still ours."

This barb wasn't directly aimed at Liverpool's John Arne Riise but in 2008 in the build up to a Derby he told the *Echo* that he had a personal interest as well as professional one in securing a win. "A few of my mates are Evertonians and they keep texting me after every game," said Riise. "So believe me when I say I truly want to beat them this weekend."

Merseyside rivalry has sometimes been put to one side when we have been reminded just what really matters in life. In 1989, Liverpool's first competitive game after the Hillsborough tragedy was a league match at Goodison. I was there that night and remember nothing of a tame 0-0 draw other than the minute's silence and a banner from the Liverpool end which read "Thanks, Everton. We Never Walked Alone" as a recognition of Blue support after the tragedy.

In 2007, the teenager Rhys Jones, a football mad-Evertonian, was shot dead in Croxteth on the outskirts of the city. The shocking crime was a big story internationally as well as locally and Liverpool FC and the fans wanted to pay their respects to Rhys and his family. Movingly, Everton's Z Cars theme was played over the PA at Anfield in a very fitting gesture.

Yin and Yang, Red and Blue, sweet and sour… football would be dull if we are all saw it through from the same perspective. Not that there is ever any chance of that happening on Merseyside.

—∿—

The other, other lot – Liverpool and Manchester United fans

Long before the Premier League was conceived, there was a song called 'Football Crazy'. The lyrics were "football robbed him of the wee bit of sense he had." Nowadays, the marketers spend a lot of time and money promoting fanaticism. The posters often show images of fans with bulging eyes, roaring on their heroes from the stands or acting like madmen after cheering a goal in the pub. There will also be inclusive images of fans with different colour replica shirts walking to the ground. "We understand your passion, because we feel the same," is the insincere message. All these sponsors, TV stations etc are just as big followers of the game as we are.

Then there are the fans who want to tell the world just how much they love their club. At Old Trafford in the Stretford End there is a banner that states: "Utd, kids, wife." Glad we know Devoted of Didsbury's life priorities.

If Liverpool and Everton fans have a family quarrel, the Reds of Merseyside and Manchester are more like neighbours who can't stand each and have to be kept apart at the local barbecue in case they spoil it for everyone else. Bad blood? The former Manchester United manager, Liverpool-born Ron Atkinson was only partly overstating it when he said matches between the two sides were "like Vietnam".

And yet Merseysiders daily head east to earn a living in the rainy city and they have even formed their own informal network called SWIM (Scousers Working in Manchester).

But that's just about where the solidarity ends. Liverpool and Everton's rivalry is based just on football matters, but when you throw Manchester into the mix, inter-city disputes also surface. Scousers and Mancs may work together, may fly from each other's airports even, but there is precious little North West love lost when the two sides meet on the football field.

The problem with Liverpool and Manchester as cities and football teams is there is just too much competitiveness. Both cities have a lot to shout about for the success of their industrialists, writers, musicians, politicians and comedians. But only Manchester has a scheming Glaswegian who was knighted on the basis of being a mate of former Labour Party spin doctor Alistair Campbell.

In the 2008-09 season, Rafa Benitez criticised Alex Ferguson's influence in the game (we won't call him 'Sir' in this book). In the interests of headlines and alliteration it was known as "Rafa's Rant" but in reality it was a sarcastic counterattack by the then Liverpool manager who was sick of the United boss acting like a mafia Don. My favourite bit of Rafa's written statement was when he suggested the fixture lists and administrative powers should just be handed over to Ferguson.

Ferguson's response? "I think he was an angry man (Rafa Benitez). He must have been disturbed for some reason. I think you have got to cut through the venom of it and hopefully he'll reflect and understand what he said was absolutely ridiculous."

And so it goes on. Some have argued that Liverpool and United fans should join forces to fight the negative impact of American ownership at their clubs. In the real world, such an alliance might get results and would be welcomed. In the world of North West fanaticism it is unthinkable. When polled by the Football Fans Census, four percent of Liverpool fans said they wanted United to beat Barcelona in the 2009 Champions League Final. I was astonished the supportive percentage was so high.

The rest of the country might have latched on to anti-United moods in recent years, but the Scousers have always thought that 30-odd miles is as close as they ever want to get to Manchester.

---

*There is an excellent Pathe news clip dealing with the preparations for the satellite link at Anfield. http://www.britishpathe.com/record.php?id=44601.

9.

Whose England is it anyway?

"I never forgave England for the way they treated Roger Hunt." **Anonymous Liverpool fan, Le Rouge Bar, Anfield September 2009**

Always keen for topics to get the fans talking, in the 2008-09 season Liverpool FC TV asked: "Would you rather see the Reds win the league or England win the World Cup?" The programme ran in an international week and featured pre-recorded interviews carried out at Anfield before a previous home match. In general, fans born or living on Merseyside were more likely to say that internationals were a pain, that they hoped Liverpool players all came back unscathed and that the whole thing got in the way of the important business of domestic football. Liverpool's non-Scouse followers seemed generally more tolerant of Three Lions mania. Yes, Liverpool was their number one love, but they would cheer for England, especially when Steven Gerrard and Jamie Carragher were playing.

One Liverpool fan who lives in the city was having none of this. When *LFC.tv's* presenter put the question to him on air, he snapped: "I would rather Liverpool won a throw-in than England won the World Cup." For supporters such as this, the hype, circus and hypocrisy that surrounds the England team is a turn-off. They don't see England but London FC, an alien concept that has nothing to do with them. Such fans loathe the band that plays the 'Great Escape', JT, the national anthem. And as for flags of St George flown from cars...

In the final home match of the 2009-10 season, travelling Chelsea fans, revelling in the glow of a 2-0 win, sang: "There's only one England captain" in praise of John Terry who had the armband taken off him for his behaviour off the pitch. The Kop, sullen and worried about matters on the field and in the boardroom, responded by telling the Londoners where they could stick "their" Three Lions before chanting "We're Not English we are Scouse."

Which is a good point to introduce you to a group of Liverpool fans who have set up the Scouse Not English website. I met Richie Greaves and his mates before a match in 2009-10 and asked them to explain why there was such a wave of indifference towards the England football team. Have they been going around stirring up apathy? Richie has shown there is a hardcore of sceptics about the national side and his website offers Scouse Not English merchandise for fans of all ages. They are not bitter, the site is more a statement of where their football priorities lie. In the aftermath of England's disastrous 2010 World Cup performances, there were many journalists who argued that Premier League football should take a back seat to help the national side flourish. If you were to express this opinion on Scouse Not English's online forum you would get a different take on the club or country debate. Many of the Scouse Not

English followers would no doubt remind you that the ambivalence cuts both ways as Liverpool players have borne the brunt of criticism over the years when they have been on England duty. The worst case was the booing of John Barnes in the early 1990s, but others with longer memories reckon Roger Hunt, who was a hero among Liverpool fans in the 1960s, was never fully appreciated outside Merseyside, despite being a World Cup winner. Another more recent indication is the media and public attitude towards Emile Heskey. In 2001 Heskey was scoring regularly for Liverpool and he was on target in a 5-1 win against Germany when all the goals came from Anfield players. But the next year when watching the World Cup on TV, I had many an argument with London work colleagues who didn't have a good word to say about him. After Heskey left Liverpool (and stopped scoring goals) he became a crucial partner for Wayne Rooney, according to the media.

Scouse Not English reckon that the irritation with the England team is based on a clash of cultures. They point out that Liverpool supporters have often sought inspiration from Europe rather than their other English fans. One quick example, Liverpool fans sang 'Allez Les Rouges' in 1977 when they played St Etienne in an unforgettable European Cup tie and when we used to win things we always sang 'Campione' and not the ridiculous Anglicisation of 'Champione'. Scouse Not English's members also told me that they feel they have nothing in common personally with other football team's followers. "We just support our team in a different way," they said. It wasn't a case of arrogance or aloofness, simply a feeling that Liverpool have their own way of doing things. You can add to that the tabloid press hyping up the national team, despite previous underachievement, a vacuous celebrity attachment towards England and a distaste of supporting players who are on the payroll of Manchester United and Chelsea. It would appear Scouse Not English make a strong case when they say the Three Lions are hard to love.

Richard Buxton, writing on the Click Liverpool website shortly before the 2010 World Cup, admitted he was very dubious about the whole spectacle. He wrote: "England in a major tournament gives any attention seeker, loudmouth or delinquent the perfect opportunity to carry out their idiocy in public with very few repercussions because they are backing the boys. If you aren't riding on the crest of this wave of national hysteria or, God forbid, if you take more interest in the fitness of your own club's players at these tournaments over the national side's fortunes, you are considered unpatriotic. Unfortunately not everyone sings from the same hymn sheet as Team Ingerlund (sic). Not everyone will stand arms outspread in the middle of the pub bellowing out 'Gawd Save The Queen'."

There is nothing new about this. When I was at school in Liverpool in the 1970s I was always conscious of how Everton and Liverpool fans became keener on the national side only if players from their club were playing. In 1977 there was a sense of pride that seven Liverpool players were in Ron Greenwood's England team. But three years later, I remember Wales thrashing England 4-1 at Wrexham in a Home International played at the end of the season. I watched the game with my mate and his dad at their home in Norris Green, about a mile and a half from Anfield, and they both found the result and the manner of England's defeat hilarious. In 1988 many Liverpool fans were delighted that one of their players, Ray Houghton, scored for Ireland against England in the European Championships.

Fast forward to 2010 and a group of Liverpool fans were among 71 supporters on a trip to Mönchengladbach (covered in a previous chapter). Being generous types, the German hosts laid on an impressive party and played Skinner and Baddiel's Euro 96 anthem 'Football's Coming Home' (later cleverly adapted by the Germans who sang 'England's going home' after the 4-1 win in the World Cup). The lads, fuelled by plenty of the local brew, joined in of course but one immediately confided: "I don't know why I am singing along to this, I fuckin' hate England!"

And that may seem to sum up Liverpool's complicated relationship with the rest of the country. Liverpool, which traditionally looked to Ireland and America for cultural inspiration, has long been assumed to be the most un-English of English cities. People from other places are only half joking when they say they "need a passport" to go to Merseyside. In the 1980s, when Margaret Thatcher was Prime Minister, the estrangement was at its worst when it often seemed like it was Scousers v the rest. Many people living in the city of Liverpool are fed-up with criticism from outsiders. A number of journalists – most notoriously the current London mayor Boris Johnson – have attacked Scousers in print. One online message from a Scouser before the 2010 World Cup suggested it was a case of: "Right then you horrible, thieving Scouse so-and-sos, it's time to support YOUR country."

But while all this may be valid it is only one half of the story. Before England's 2010 "campaign" descended into fiasco, elimination and acrimony there were plenty of St George flags in Liverpool, just as there were in Lincoln, London and Launceston. One of the first things one saw in early June 2010 on coming out of Lime Street station was a huge England flag in the Punch and Judy pub. Before the tournament Liverpool's bin men complained to the *Liverpool Echo* that they weren't allowed to display national flags of St George on their wagons (arguably, a rather appropriate place to put them). Many of the callers to BBC radio phone-ins after England's draws against the United States and Algeria were Scousers clearly wishing Fabio Capello's players well in South Africa, despite all the disappointment and soap opera of that tournament. To help us understand the other side, let's hear from Rob Taubman.

Now, in the interests of transparency Rob, a 52-year-old from Anfield, was interviewed for this book several months before the blunders of Bloemfontein and the events of that match with Germany would be enough to depress the most committed England fan. But as with his club, his football loyalties go way back. He said: "There have always been Liverpool supporters at England games. I first started going to England games in 1982 with a gang of lads, half Liverpool and half Everton, from Fazakerley, to the World Cup in Spain. Apart from the Londoners, the next biggest group of fans there were from Liverpool. Englandfans published the list of clubs supported by England fans. Liverpool are second and United are first.

"There are about 40 members of Scouse Not English, but there are something like 5,000 members of the England fan club – which you have to pay £65 to be a member of – who are Liverpool supporters. So if you are talking democracy and you took a vote, it would be a landslide (in favour of England). There is a section of England fans who are so utterly naïve it is beyond belief. On the forums they were saying Gerrard should have his (hernia) operation now so he will be fit for the World Cup in South Africa. You say to them 'do you realise you are talking absolute balderdash? His wages are paid by Liverpool Football Club and England borrow players.' England play no part in bringing them forward, no part in the development nor the coaching. They borrow them and send them back injured. I can see that.

"But England have a lot of support among your Rochdales, your Brentfords etc. One of the things that shows the lower league mentality of the England fans and their naivety is when we play away from home, you will find a fan in your seat and you will tell them and they will reply 'oh just sit anywhere, mate.' I say 'no, you go and sit anywhere, you are in my seat.' The reason is that when you go to Rochdale it doesn't really matter where you sit. You go to Anfield or Old Trafford and just sit where you like and see how far you get."

Taubman said that the cost of following England to South Africa was about £4,000 and while many Reds would not consider parting with a tenth of this to watch England, he believes it is ridiculous to suggest that we must choose club or country, but not both.

"When England were playing games at Old Trafford we used to get the train and the last one coming back to Lime Street was heaving. England played Poland in a qualifier and it was standing room only. I am usually not here when there is a big tournament, but if everyone in Liverpool is supposed to hate England why is it that when the World Cup starts there are hundreds and hundreds of cars with the cross of St George? And why not? You should show support for your country. I didn't go to Japan and South Korea but I did see the streets of Liverpool deserted every time England played. They had pictures of Tithebarn Street at 8.30 in the morning. The country came to a standstill.

"The night we beat Argentina (2002) there were gangs of drunks in town singing 'England' everywhere. They were the same people who were saying three weeks earlier that they weren't interested. It's not cool to support England for them. A few years ago it seemed to be cool to support Ireland. I would ask 'why?' and they would say 'because my granddad was Irish.' I would say 'yeah, but you're not.'

"Pick anything and you will find people who don't like it. Among England fans, Liverpool aren't really known for it (hostility) but United are. United take it to extremes because after Croatia beat England in 2007, United fans had Croatia's flag at Bolton in the ground. Liverpool fans don't do anything like that. At Anfield, you get 20 people with an anti-England song. Not that I have ever heard it and I go on the Kop. I have heard them sing 'we're not English, we are Scouse.' But of the other 40,000 at Anfield 1% will say I go to England games and the other 99% will at least watch England on TV. It is a vociferous minority."

And then there is Neil Rodgers, 46, who comes from Huyton and is married with teenaged sons. He freely admits his family thinks he is crackers for his football allegiance – Liverpool and Russia. "Who do I support when Russia play England? This is simple…Russia. Our club travelled to London for the Euro 2008 qualifier and sat with the Russian supporters in Wembley Stadium. I won't mention the result... I got a lot of stick from my mates when (Arsenal's Andriy) Arshavin scored four past us at Anfield. I personally don't support England as England have always been based in London. The FA had a chance to build the new stadium outside of London. The midlands would have been ideal but no they went ahead and built it in London. I was absolutely gutted when Russia didn't get to the World Cup Finals in 2010. The first leg in Moscow, Russia needed a two-goal advantage to go into the second leg in Slovenia, but Slovenia scored a late goal to make it 2-1. In my opinion the Russian players were under so much pressure, they just couldn't score the goal they needed. Slovenia played the better football over the two legs so I can't complain. Now I am looking forward to the Euros in 2012."

International football is a blessing and a curse and I have to admit that in my lifetime I have watched England live five times, including two matches in the 1988 European Championships in Germany. It's highly likely that I won't make it to six. I would have no hesitation in spending a lot of money to watch Liverpool play in Europe, but I would think twice about watching England if you offered me a free ticket. This is not through any anti-Englishness. After all I was born in England and have lived here all my life. I am very interested in watching England on TV when they are involved in genuinely big games such as Germany in the World Cup, but I just don't share the enthusiasm of others around the country. Is it simply a case that the national team just isn't special enough for certain

Liverpool fans? Maybe there is only so much passion and loyalty to go around.

Rob Taubman is correct in suggesting support for England on the Kop is underestimated, but the Scouse Not English lads also have a point when they say that many Liverpool fans just don't "do" England. After England flopped so badly in South Africa, only the most loyal will follow them to Ukraine and Poland if they reach the Euro 2012 finals. Good luck to them. Like Taubman, they are genuine football fans who deserve respect for their commitment to the cause. But in the summer of 2012, sports fans and assorted hangers on and glory seekers will be distracted by the build-up to the Olympics. Even occasional football watchers who cheer for England because everyone else is doing so, will remember how they were taken in by the hype of 2010 and think twice before sticking a flag on the windscreen.

For many, the 2010 World Cup final posed questions about the Netherlands' rough tactics or Howard Webb's refereeing. For Anfield regulars, the most significant moment of the two hours was seeing Fernando Torres pull up with an injury towards the end of extra time. When this happened we did what we always do when discussing international football...we asked: "What does this mean for Liverpool?"

10.

A Show of Red strength: the importance of Asia

"Liverpool has not come to play football as much as bring footballers to play salesmen." **Rohit Brijnath, Straits Times, Singapore, 2009**

Liverpool's plan for growth could be summed up in one important four letter word – Asia. This vast continent of 3.8billion people is home to 56% of the world's population and provides exciting opportunities for sponsorship, merchandise, new support, revenue from internet subscriptions and other assorted spin offs. Everyone wants a piece of the action and despite boardroom chaos in recent years, the Anfield hierarchy has been consistent in its policy of trying to "crack" the Asian market. As any football marketing person knows, the opportunities and potential for success in Asia is matched only by the challenges faced in "building a brand" there. Asia can prove to be the most lucrative of all cash cows, but it is a tough job to milk it.

A cynical start to the chapter, I confess, and before we go on it may be a good idea to remember why there is a potential Asian market for Liverpool to exploit in the first place. Throughout the 2009-10 season, I received regular email updates from a fan called Boo Soon Yew who edits the website for his branch, the Official Liverpool Supporters Club of Malaysia, one of 18 officially accredited by LFC's Association of International Branches in Asia. Boo's rallying calls to "fellow Reds" were a welcome lift from the gloom of events at home. In Malaysia there are 1,200 active members with an average age of 34 and for many of them, supporting Liverpool is a way of life.

Boo said: "I became a Liverpool fan when I was maybe seven or eight years old when I started reading newspapers in the late 1970s. I was fascinated with this team that topped the English Division One. Then, with the advent of TV and 'Big League Soccer', I was able to enjoy the free-flowing football from this team in red called Liverpool. My wish is to see our Liverpool fan base expand…not just in Merseyside or England but also the whole world. The age of technology and the internet has smashed boundaries and now we are just a few clicks away from expressing our thoughts to one another. LFC Facebook is an excellent step to reach out to fans individually. Now I look forward to a more co-ordinated effort between Liverpool FC and the official overseas branches."

As Boo said, the internet provides a lifeline for Liverpool's Asian-based fans, many of whom are expats who have moved about 6,000 miles to start a new life but still want to follow their team as closely as they can. This used to be all but impossible, particularly in China which has undergone one of the biggest and quickest economic transformations of any country in history. And like everywhere else, China has embraced the concept of the sports bar.

In May 2009 I was in Shanghai on work unconnected with this book when I saw an internet advertisement for the Hard Day's Night Bar in the city. Shanghai is a stunning, futuristic port in Eastern China and it has long been a major trading post, but now this metropolis of 20-odd million people feels as if it is the centre of the world. Imagine a Liverpool and Wirral setting and multiply it by 40 and you get some idea of the lay-out of Shanghai. Comparing Liverpool with Shanghai is no accident, either. The cities have historical connections and are both twinned. Liverpool was strongly represented at World Expo in 2010, the so-called Olympic Games for business, which was held in Shanghai.

As for The Hard Day's Night, it is on the "Wirral" or Pudong side of the Huangpu River. It's something of a traveller cliché to say my taxi driver was a bit too quick for comfort. But the one who took me to the bar seemed to have modelled his driving on Michael Schumacher during the German's more reckless days. By the time I reached the bar, we had been driving for an hour, had covered plenty of miles and yet were still in the city. You get used to that in Shanghai.

In need of a cold beer and a meal I was greeted by Jim Burton, co owner of the bar and a Liverpool supporter who went to work at Plessey's Edge Lane plant on Merseyside at the age of 16 before rising to managing director level in telecommunications in Asia. Then he decided he wanted a change of direction and now runs a Beatle-themed venue which features live music and plenty of Premier League football. The walls are decked with pictures of Liverpool players, although Jim says he has no problem in playing mine host to Manchester United fans, provided they get the cash tills ringing. The bar also has traditional English fare on the menu and I have to admit that I did order the Hard Day's Night's own speciality, Scouse.

For Burton and his business partner, also a Liverpool supporter, from the city's Wavertree area, the Hard Day's Night offers some reminders of the old country and it is no coincidence that they use football to promote the bar. "I was sent to China for the first time in 1986 to do sales engineering support," said Burton. "You would still see the grey Chairman Mao suits which were the majority dress. It was a culture shock, but it didn't take me long to like it. I liked the fact it was different – it was a challenge.

"In the last five years interest in Liverpool has grown among the Chinese and they are very well informed. Everybody knows Liverpool. They started getting interested around the time of Istanbul. That is one of the best games anyone could hope to watch. If you say you are a Liverpool supporter they will recount that game. That was on Chinese TV at 2am in the morning. Those who didn't watch it live saw the headlines. It was a big deal, bigger than the World Cup. If it wasn't for Istanbul you would have a few more Man United fans in China. A game like that draws you in. If you didn't know who to support before, that draws you in."

A major obstacle to English clubs making money in China is fake merchandise. No sooner do teams reveal a new strip, it is being copied somewhere and being sold at prices that undercut the major stores. Burton said:

"You go down to the market and buy 22 football kits for the price of a genuine one. A full kit is £80-£90. It is a big issue and no-one does much about it. I think if Liverpool opened a shop it would get a lot of hits, not necessarily for kits, but for things you can't get at the market. Counterfeiting is happening anyway, but no team is getting any sales.

"In China you don't see a step change – it is gradual. For a long time there has always been a small interest. You would sit around the banquet table and they will know something about sport and football. The level of detail has got more and more over the years. Like anything in China, it's a case of gradual development."

The Premier League has a popular "global" product and Asia has a growing number of young professional people with money to spend. Advertisements in Asian languages are regularly seen on perimeter advertisements at Premier League grounds and the Saturday lunch time kick off times were introduced partly for the Eastern markets who are about seven hours ahead of UK time.

So it does seem like the proverbial no brainer. Football clubs want to break into new markets and China is a country with a lot of potential everything, especially sports fans with disposable cash from the economic growth. But life is not that simple and in his book *Bamboo Goalposts*, Rowan Simons, who is an expert on football in the People's Republic, said there are a number of reasons why English Premier League clubs have not made the money they may have hoped for. Simons reckoned Liverpool were well positioned to cash in just as China was opening itself out to the rest of the world. In 2000-2001 there was a project called 'Liverpool in China' which involved Ian Rush visiting football academies and signing autographs. But there are reasons why the Premier League has found success elusive in China, despite the fanfare. According to Simons, there has been no co-ordinated involvement of the Premier League. Instead, it has been a case individual clubs trying to grab their slice of the pie. Second, Chinese football fans have sometimes followed clubs based on personal support for one player. I have heard it said that in Shenzen or Beijing, a fan whose favourite player is Michael Owen might switch allegiance from Liverpool (in 2004) to Man United (2009) and this would be perfectly acceptable. To do this in England with our tribal team loyalties would bring scorn. Finally, Chinese sports fans are keen on basketball and might be more prepared to take their lead from US sports than English ones.

Forward thinking and innovation are also no guarantee of success, according to Simons. He wrote: "My best advice to the Premier Leaguers that come around from time to time was that, unless football clubs could lose the ego and work together 'for the real good of the game' by supporting the grassroots over the long term, they should limit the damage by spending as little money and resources on China as possible. It makes me very sad, but the foreign clubs which had yet to invest in China at the turn of the 21st century were well ahead of the game; they had yet to make any mistakes. Sports brands, just like any other products, have to work hard to secure customer loyalty and China has very little of that."

Nick Harris, a British sports journalist and writer, argued in his book *The Foreign Revolution* that there is "a huge, if fickle, interest in football in China". Harris warns that Sheffield United's sporting links with

Chengdu, a city of 10million people, were seen as being of huge significance at the time, but they haven't been reflected in genuine commercial revenue. "China appeared in the 2002 World Cup. Lots of people thought they could make money but there are lots chasing not as much cash as they thought and outside the biggest cities it is even trickier," Harris wrote.

None of this will be news to Ian Ayre, who became Liverpool FC's commercial director in 2007. Before his appointment, Ayre's main claim to fame at Anfield was scoring a penalty in front of the Kop as a schoolboy during a testimonial match and cheering his team on from the terraces. Ayre, who is in his 40s, left Litherland High School at 16 to join the navy and then did very nicely selling set top boxes in Asia. He went on to become chief executive of Total Sports Asia and Huddersfield Town. Since his appointment, in all interviews he mentions Asia as being of huge strategic interest to Liverpool FC and this point was reinforced in comments reported by the blogger David Tully on Liverpool4Life. "The football is on everywhere in Asia – people gather to watch it at night in bars, restaurants and other places, everywhere. That speaks volumes for the size of the appetite and we have got a system, a process and a partnership in place to serve that," Ayre said.

Liverpool FC's sponsorship deal with Standard Chartered which began at the start of the 2010-11 season was also significant. Not only were Standard Chartered only the second club to sponsor LFC in the Premier League era, they too have key business interests in Asia.

The same blog article by Tully suggested that Liverpool have 58million fans in China, 6m in India, 5m in Thailand, 2m in Malaysia and 2m in Japan. That would amount to an impressive 75million Liverpool "supporters" in Asia, but such figures are impossible to prove or disprove. It does suggest there is a potential gold mine for "Brand Liverpool" which needs to secure greater market share abroad to satisfy the club's ambitions back home. But how can we quantify just who does and doesn't support Liverpool? How do you define a fan, anyway? Is it someone who takes an active interest and spends money which goes directly to the club? If so, we can reduce that 75million figure dramatically.

What is certain is that Liverpool's 2009 pre-season tour set a new benchmark for the club's activities in Asia. 'The Kop Comes to Asia' was the official title of an event that was part rock tour and part warm-up for what proved to be a disastrous season. In 2009, LFC TV showed a special documentary marking Liverpool's pre-season tour which involved matches in Thailand and Singapore.

Jamie Carragher was in no doubt that the goodwill trip was of importance and he told *LFC.tv:* "We should be proud of the fact that our club is so big out here." For Kenny Dalglish it was his first trip in his role which began as ambassador and developed into something much more wide ranging, and he said: "It just opens your eyes to the support and the feeling there is for Liverpool Football Club."

The tour was organised by former Anfield hardman of the 1980s Steve McMahon's Profitable Group and the Thais were managed at the time by Peter Reid, a boyhood Kopite who went on to be McMahon's fiercest rival playing for Everton. McMahon is now a television pundit in Asia and can see there is great potential for Liverpool to expand in his new adopted continent.

McMahon told *LFC.tv*: "I played for Liverpool and captained them, but the next best thing is to bring them to Asia. The reception was fantastic and it shows Liverpool people there is a big, bad world out there. I have been in Asia for four years and everywhere you go you see support for Liverpool."

During the trip, Dirk Kuyt and Dalglish hosted an adidas coaching session for 150 Thai youngsters.

Then it was on to Singapore where Liverpool were greeted with even more fervour as they sailed through a river in the city. Gerrard was missing as he had to appear in court on Merseyside where he was cleared of an affray charge. A banner summed up the deep level of devotion from fans who don't often get the chance to see their idols in the flesh. It read: "Someday we will find the words to describe our appreciation. For now we will simply say that you are our inspiration. From your fans in Singapore, You'll Never Walk Alone."

LFC TV presenter Claire Rourke said that regular match goers would look on in bewilderment or amusement at this. Do we take it for granted? she wondered. Liverpool won the Merlion Cup and stand-in Carragher looked slightly embarrassed on the podium after the game, although maybe we should not have looked this particular gift horse in the mouth as it was all we won that season.

Watching all this Mersey mania was a son of Kirkby, Keith Moore, who made the 8,000-mile round trip from Sydney to watch Liverpool on their pre-season Asian tour. Moore moved to Australia in 1980 as one of the last "£10 Poms" who were given an assisted passage

Down Under. He has settled in Australia and has kept his Scouse accent even though these days he only returns to the UK once a year to see family and take in some matches at Anfield.

He said: "I got two VIP tickets to watch Liverpool train. I met the Profitable Group who organised the tour and asked 'could you get them out to Sydney?' But the distance is the problem. It takes all week to get over the flight to and from England. Going there in the close season just isn't viable and that's why a lot of teams don't come to Australia. They used to a few years ago, but they know the big market is Asia. That's why they will go to Malaysia, Korea etc. Liverpool know the bread and butter is Asia. That boat trip with the team down the river was when we were there in Singapore. It was fantastic. We were on the Cavern bar on the River. I got two VIP passes and met the players at the end of a training session. I met Kenny Dalglish, Rafa, Torres. Torres was just like a little kid, very shy.

"The passion of the people in Singapore was fantastic. I had never heard 'You'll Never Walk Alone' sung like that. I was with my mate and we were in this bar and they were showing the St Etienne game from 1977. We were talking about the game because we were in the Anfield Road End for that. There was an Indian fella near us and he said 'were you guys at this game?' We told him we were and he asked how many other games we had been to. I said, 'in the seventies, mate, about 300.'

"We are quite blasé about going to the game, but for people in Asia it is a once in a lifetime thing. They never go."

But it wasn't all sweetness and light on this goodwill

tour. Behind the smiles and the five-star air conditioned receptions for the players and coaches, the Asian public were understandably keen to know just why Torres and Gerrard – the two star turns – were not able to travel with the squad. Gerrard was involved in a court case at the time and Torres was rested after international duty with Spain in the Confederations Cup. It is one of the realities of modern sport that fans want to see the stars, but the stars have many demands on their time and body and something has to give.

Not that this cut much ice with fans who had filled grounds and paid Premier League ticket prices to get a rare glimpse of players who weren't able to play. Writing in the Singapore newspaper the *Straits Times*, Rohit Brjinath suggested that the locals had not been given value for money. He wrote: "Friendly matches are strolls in the park. We know this, we cannot claim surprise here. Liverpool has not come to play football as much as bring footballers to play salesman. But it is one thing for a match to be an acceptable fake, another thing for it to become an unacceptable farce. This is the fine line friendlies walk: we know it's about business, but some pretence to the contrary needs to be maintained."

He added: "This seems like unfortunate timing, pure bad luck, yet for the fan it's also like paying $88, or $188, and finding that the Beatles didn't bring John Lennon and Paul McCartney has a runny nose. If the field is empty of stars, or interested footballers, tomorrow, it will be fair to feel disappointed with the organisers."

For all that, Liverpool already have a devoted following in the Far East and so many of the fans in Asia are doing their bit to enhance Liverpool's standing in the world game. One example of this is seen in Thailand where the Bangkok branch has organised friendly soccer matches and charitable work including donating blood to the Thai Red Cross Society and holding free lunch parties for local orphans. In 2003, Thai newspaper *The Nation* reported how a 17-year-old student Kannita Sunsee, had renamed herself 'Alone' from 'You'll Never Walk Alone' "Because I like this song and I just want this name to represent myself as one of Liverpool's real fans," she said.

Ian Ayre isn't the first Liverpool FC executive to understand the importance of Asia and he probably won't be the last. But how effectively will he be able to transfer all this opportunity and Eastern promise into hard cash?

11.

Our famous atmosphere

"Let's not dilute what we've got, a culture we can be proud of, a culture we can boast about and be the envy of others instead of being the same." **Reclaim the Kop charter, 2007**

Not only can Liverpool FC fans claim the most famous stand in world football and some of the wittiest and most creative banners ever seen, they are unique for having their own code of practice. Yes, Liverpool fans who are not sure how to support the team, were given some help, thanks to the Reclaim the Kop campaign.

Before we look at this further, it's helpful to consider some recent history. When the Premier League was formed in 1992 it was presented as a whole new ball game, a fresh start for the national sport. But for many Liverpool supporters, the past had included an unparalleled record of success. Nationally, many spoke of reigniting interest in football in the early 1990s, but even in the 1980s, during times of economic crisis and despite LFC's involvement in two tragedies, the game was in rude health on Merseyside. It dominates discussion now but it was huge a generation ago and a generation before that. When Liverpool first brought the FA Cup back from London in 1965, half a million people lined the streets and the city was brought to a standstill. Forty years later when Liverpool paraded the European Cup, in town the fervour was arguably greater, but that was possibly the most cherished event in the club's illustrious history.

The Miracle of Istanbul and the great European nights of the Benitez era at Anfield persuaded fans from around the world that something special happens at the ground on match days. Make that certain match days because often there is a distinct lack of atmosphere at the ground for the workaday Premier League clash. If Liverpool are doing OK but not great there will be a quiet contentment, but sometimes it takes the opposition scoring to raise the noise levels.

It is possible to trace all this back to the turn of the millennium and before. Many people unfairly blame it on out-of-towners who "don't know traditions of Liverpool". This ignores the fact that when Liverpool played Chelsea in the Champions League semi-final in 2005 on a night generally regarded as one of the noisiest ever at Anfield, many of those bellowing their support were from Ireland, Europe and all parts of the UK. I know, I heard them near me in the ground. And don't forget there have been many times during dull games when local fans have sat there in a stony silence with arms folded, particularly in recent years.

It does feel that sections of Liverpool fans from all birthplaces have been encouraged to be consumers rather than partisan followers of their team and it does appear that short term interests come into play. A Merseyside based season ticket holder who has been following

Liverpool for decades may drink in a local pub and take his place on the Kop 15 minutes before kick-off. He may not buy a programme and may leave the ground swiftly to meet his mates for a drink and a post-mortem of the 90 minutes afterwards. In contrast, a fan making a first or a rare visit to Anfield may want to buy more merchandise and soak up the atmosphere. They may be keener to video the fans singing 'You'll Never Walk Alone' so they can upload it on to YouTube rather than just joining in. The first fan has invested thousands – even tens of thousands – of pounds following Liverpool over the years. But he or she isn't as "high yield" on a match day as the one-off visitor. It was put to me in very plausible terms by a Manchester United fan and work colleague who once said: "Sixty-odd thousand Koreans making their first trip to Old Trafford are always going to spend more than 60,000 lads from Salford and Manchester. Who would you want in the ground when it's all about making money? It's the same at Liverpool only your ground's smaller."

The switch to an all-seater stadium in the mid-1990s was a significant landmark for those who believe Anfield has lost some of its old magic. In 2002, the *Liverpool Echo*'s letters pages even debated whether it was time to introduce a residency ruling with Scousers only being allowed in certain sections. One correspondent Mick, from Liverpool, said this should be the case.

But Tony, also from Liverpool, hit the nail on the head. "How does anyone work out that tickets for any section of the ground should only be available to people who live in Liverpool? There are two very good reasons not to do this. One, the population of this country is now much more mobile and having lived in numerous parts of the country I hear many Scouse accents everywhere I go – so, if you move away from Liverpool you shouldn't be allowed to go to the game?"

And Paul Winrow, a Reds fan from Ipswich, suggested that without the non-Scouse support, Liverpool would average less than 25,000 per home match.

Five years after this debate, Reclaim the Kop, described by the *Echo* as a "grassroots campaign to restore old values of crowd support at Anfield", was born. Liverpool FC gave their official blessing with then Chief Executive Rick Parry saying: "Any initiative to further improve the match day atmosphere is to be warmly welcomed." There was no doubt a feeling in the corridors of power that Reclaim the Kop offered more opportunities than risks. In January 2007 the charter was presented which contained 10 points or principles of being a Liverpool supporter. It is worth looking at these in more detail.

First, the charter said that Kopites are custodians of the stand and that no individual owns or is bigger than "the spirit" of the place. There was also a lot of significance given to Liverpool fans' uniqueness. "There is no other," said the charter and it made the point that The Kop is a source of innovation in football support. There were pledges to get behind the team at all times and to never argue about the merits of Liverpool players. Applauding the goalkeeper when he runs to the Kop end – a long-time Anfield tradition – was also included. Interestingly, RTK called for fans to get to the ground earlier "we want the opposition shrivelling". Respect for the memory of those who died at Hillsborough was prominent as was a pledge never to buy *The Sun* newspaper. RTK also pleaded for tolerance, both for Scousers towards out of town followers and vice versa.

"It's not clever to laugh along with away fans who sing tiresome nursery rhymes about car crime. Support Liverpool FC and you support Liverpool too." Finally, RTK stated that racism should not be tolerated and that 'You'll Never Walk Alone' should be sung as a "hymn of triumph." "Let's not dilute what we've got, a culture we can be proud of, a culture we can boast about and be the envy of others instead of being the same."

RTK then followed the charter a year later with a 'Keep Flags Scouse' campaign. A statement said: "The banners are just another cog in the Liverpool tradition machine of being different, being unique and being special. The Keep Flags Scouse campaign came about to try and protect this tradition…and keep the new fans travelling with us informed." Definitely not welcomed by the Keep Flags Scouse campaign were the unimaginative flags of St George which are favoured by other English clubs on European trips. In fact, Liverpool's support has long been visual as well as vocal. Many of the fans' banners are works of art, ranging from witty plays on words to famous quotations and – during the 2007 Champions League final in Athens – Greek philosophy. In recent seasons, Liverpool fans have produced magnificent examples of art work with pictures of managers and players prominent. What other club could bring out an entire book based on famous banners? Of course, the greatest ever Liverpool banner remains the 1977 masterpiece in honour of Joey Jones – "Joey Ate The Frogs Legs, Made The Swiss Roll, Now He's Munching Gladbach."

Andy Knott, a 42-year-old from St Helens, has been doing his bit over the years to make Anfield visually arresting. Once or twice a season, Knott, an art technician at a high school, helps organise giant mosaics on the Kop. The mosaics have paid tribute to Liverpool legends from Bill Shankly to Sami Hyypia and have also included serious issues such as the Hillsborough Justice Campaign and the Free Michael Shields protest. A typical mosaic covers 12,500 seats, going back 74 rows in the steepest parts of the Kop. It costs about £1,500 to make a mosaic and is a labour of love as it can take from two hours to a full day to lay all the cards on the seats. It shows the level of commitment among the fans that the mosaics always seem to work and the only drawback for Andy and the other Kopites is they can't see the full effect. "I feel very proud when I see the mosaics although it is usually later, like the Ray Kennedy appeal against Arsenal. We would go to the club and say 'can we do one for this?' If they agree they just say 'yes, do it' and we get on with it. There tends to be more help from volunteers when there is an issue that gets fans on the forums and that's when you get the best response – Hillsborough, for instance. We have had volunteers from Ireland, Norway, Greece, US, Malaysia – people who are over or people we know. They take a pic and they are happy. For the first Michael Shields mosaic (Free Michael) it was done on the benefit day he had at Anfield. I met his mum and dad and they were very appreciative and very proud to see it. I have never known the club to say no but they do tell us how to word it. They need to see the sheets because they don't want to see anything derogatory."

Does Andy believe The Kop is particularly suited to displaying a mosaic? "I have helped out with the Kick it Out (anti-racism) campaign at Reading, Chelsea and Stoke but the stands are not deep enough to get a good effect. The Kop is one bank of seating so it definitely lends itself to a mosaic. The mosaic is a statement that says this is how we are and it shows that the everyday fan is still there and that spirit lives on at Anfield."

But for many fans it is too late to reclaim the Kop or any other part of Anfield. These are the people who simply cannot afford to go to the match. They have seen inflation busting increases in ticket prices for more than 15 years and have had to settle for being an "armchair fan". This is an interesting term because until about 1993-94 it was used apologetically by supporters. Fans who didn't go to live football sometimes felt they had to justify themselves to others for only watching Liverpool on TV. "I would like to go more but it is difficult because of work," was a common explanation. Nowadays fans often don't have the chance to go to Anfield as they have neither the money nor the access through loyalty on fan cards or Official Club Membership to get in. As this sorry trend has developed, one of the biggest changes of all in football support has been the move to communal viewing of sport on big screens in pubs.

I have to declare an interest here. I like to concentrate on what is going on when I am watching a match on the box and this is impossible in the chaos of a crowded bar. Big screen football is often football for people who don't like football. Can we really feel part of an occasion if we are watching it on a screen with Andy Gray's commentary for company? Lifelong Red Rob Taubman put it into an interesting perspective when describing the hours before the notorious Athens "Numbers Game" Champions League final of 2007 when many Liverpool fans were unable to get tickets. Taubman said: "In Athens I met some Libyans living in Prague who told me 'We have heard so much about the fantastic support and we wanted to be part of it'. Now you if you take that to the nth degree there will be 25,000 people at a final to see the Liverpool support and there will be no Liverpool support there." They will be watching in bars, no doubt.

In other cases, supporters of Liverpool and other clubs are turning to the internet to pick up matches for free, particularly the increasingly rare Saturday 3pm kick-offs. International readers might find this difficult to believe, but often the most awkward place to watch a Liverpool match on the box sometimes is the UK. International rights mean all our matches are shown on some foreign language overseas channel and the international broadcasters are only too happy to meet the demand of Liverpool's global support. But at 3pm on a Saturday in the UK, broadcasting restrictions mean that fans are asked to tune into *Sky Sports* to watch old pros sitting in front of screens attempting to tell us what is happening. Many try to avoid this nonsense by going to pubs which have unofficially "converted" their aerials to beam in coverage from Saudi Arabia, Scandinavia or anywhere else where the Liverpool game is being shown. But as the regulators have clamped down that option has been closed off and there has been an increase in the use of shadowy websites which screen matches. These are all well and good but the viewing experience is ruined by the screen freezing constantly. Surely, in years to come, we will look back and laugh at some of the stupid restrictions placed on football fans who just want to watch their own team play all their Premier League games live.

We can't let this chapter go without tackling a particular talking point among Liverpool fans. Wearing a jester's hat would certainly be a violation of the Reclaim the Kop charter and it is such a gauche and un-Liverpool thing to do that Scouse poet and lifelong Red Dave Kirby wrote a whole poem on the subject. For Kirby, the jester's hat symbolises a lot that is wrong with the modern game. Such monstrosities are worn by the terminally unaware who think they are being wacky. Kirby, whose verses have chronicled the changing face of Liverpool's match day support, looks back fondly to the time before such headwear was seen at Anfield.

Another Liverpool fan, who used the internet name of Crazy Horse in tribute to Liverpool legend Emlyn Hughes, put it even more bluntly. "I've met a lot of good people who support the Reds, from all over the world. I just hate all the knobheads that are attracted to the club. When the football bubble bursts and it's not fashionable to watch football anymore they will all just F**k off back to the stones they crawled from, leaving true fans to enjoy the game and club that is a part of them. And there won't be a F***ing jester hat in sight!"

12.

Cheering for the shirt

"We all dream of a team of Carraghers." **Kop chant to the tune of Yellow Submarine**

How can a working class bloke from Speke or Kirkdale relate to a footballer on £90,000 a week? Do the men in the first team squad, employees of Liverpool Football Club, have anything in common with the common man these days? These were questions on my mind as I did something I wouldn't normally do and went to a testimonial match at Anfield in September 2010.

On my personal list of must-see events, testimonials generally rank just a little higher than the latest Katie Price book launch or Jedward's gigs. I like my football competitive at Anfield and the artificial nature of these games is a killer for me. Some reckon the testimonial is a way of saying thanks to players for their service while others argue that's what we do anyway by going to matches, buying merchandise and cheering from the stands. But I was happy to pay £20 just this once to see Jamie Carragher's benefit match at Anfield. And much as I admire Carra, it's quite possible that I would have opted to stay at home if it wasn't for Niall Quinn.

In 2002, Quinn, now the chairman of Sunderland but then still a player, showed that footballers can give something back to the community by handing over the gate receipts from his testimonial to local charities. Apparently, it was typical of Quinn who has been known to pay out from his own pocket to help stranded fans get back from away matches. The former Irish international started a trend of corporate social responsibility by footballers. In fact you could call it ground breaking, the sort of gesture that threatened to give football a good name. Quinn recognised he had enjoyed a long career and had been well rewarded for his efforts on the field. Unlike the old pros from years before who earned little from being kicked for nine months of the year season after season and needed a final pay day to buy a pub or provide for their retirement, he didn't need the money from his testimonial but he knew it could be put to good use elsewhere.

It is a model that Carragher updated for his testimonial and money raised from a special match against Everton at Anfield went to his 23 Foundation which supports children's charities on Merseyside. On his website www.jamiecarragher23.co.uk, Carragher says: "At the 23 foundation we promote the idea of "we" and "us" because together as a community and with help from people like you reading this, we can accomplish anything."

Liverpool supporters would no doubt argue that Carragher is a special case. He is a local player – born in Bootle – and is the polar opposite of the stereotypical big headed Premier League star who is only interested in what he can get out of the game. Carragher takes a genuine interest in the communities he grew up in because members of his family and his friends still live in them. Carragher has become very wealthy during a decade and a bit in Liverpool's first team, but I have yet to hear anyone begrudge him his success. He has consistently given us full value for money, most notably when battling cramp to prevent Milan scoring against us in extra time in the 2005 Champions League final. One fan said to me in April 2010 when Carragher was going through an untypically poor run of form: "We know Jamie isn't playing well. But you don't say that in public, do you? It's like slagging off your own family."

The Professional Footballers' Association would no doubt argue that Carragher isn't a one-off and that many players have a social conscience. But footballers have a poor reputation for being self-serving and cynical. The Premier League has encouraged a mercenary culture in which players from the four corners of the earth kiss the badge when it suits them but run off in search of a bigger stage or a larger bundle of cash when they get a better deal. (This was made all too clear to Liverpool fans when one time badge kisser Javier Mascherano successfully agitated for a move to Barcelona at the start of the 2010-11 season.) In some cases even community work undertaken by players work looks artificial and is a way of generating favourable PR for players to build their brand.

No one could accuse Carragher of such cynicism. He has been described as the fans' representative on the pitch and the heartbeat of Liverpool FC. As supporters, we have long applauded his professionalism and his appetite to play the game in the right way. Carragher is one of the most consistent and unfussy players to have worn the red shirt. You always know what you will get from him from the moment he runs on to the field before the game when he waves to mates around the ground. You know he will be right at the heart of the action, tackling, keeping it simple, directing, encouraging and occasionally ranting at incompetence around him. Carragher is modest but also a natural competitor and in interviews reminds us that he has not featured in more than 600 games at the top level on 100 per cent commitment alone. The fella can play a bit as well.

When Milan Jovanovic and Joe Cole moved to Anfield they were also preparing to join a select club of about 700 men who can say they have done something the rest of us can only dream about – played some part of a senior match for Liverpool FC. Many of the 700 were legends (genuine ones) and others were celebrated for all sorts of reasons. In the 19th Century there was Andrew Hannah, Liverpool's first ever captain who, according to the magnificent website lfchistory.net, once walked into a lion's cage to win a £5 bet. Then there was Elisha Scott, an Irish goalkeeper, whose rivalry with Everton's greatest ever goal scorer Dixie Dean in the 1920s brought added spice to Merseyside derbies. It was said that Dean once saw Scott in the street and nodded to him to say hello. Scott flung himself full length on the pavement to stop an imaginary header. (Was this story true? Who cares?) More recently, the Dutch striker Erik Meijer, one of Gerard Houllier's signings, became a cult hero despite playing only 27 matches and scoring two goals. Meijer is remembered fondly for travelling to Dortmund on his own steam in 2001 – almost a year after he had left Anfield – and joining the Liverpool fans for a session on the beer at the fans' party before the UEFA Cup final.

Meijer is hardly typical and his laddish mixing was notable because it was so rare. In many other cases fans have found it difficult to relate to players. We talk about Carragher, Gerrard and others but lower down the cast list the likes of Albert Riera, Jermaine Pennant, Josemi and others have struggled to win a place in the hearts of the fans. That might not be their fault and not all footballers have to be raconteurs or backslappers. But the likes of Pennant and others with their ridiculous coloured boots and underachievement on the pitch did seem to believe they had made it simply by joining Liverpool.

Keith Moore, who left his home in Kirkby to live in Sydney, Australia in 1980, had a welcome reminder of an era when players still felt like one of us. Moore returns to his native Merseyside once a year to visit family and watch some matches. In 2009 he was joined by an Australian-based friend, Bill Londos, whose life's ambition was to see Liverpool play at Anfield. "I sorted him out with tickets for the Stoke game," said Moore. "He made the journey up from London on the day and I met him at Lime Street. We were walking up to the Liverpool supporters' shop in Williamson Square and we saw Jimmy Case. I had a chat with Jimmy and explained who we were. I took Bill all around Liverpool, to Jamie Carragher's bar. He was amazed at all the pictures. Bill had been in London and it was very unfriendly. He said afterwards I am going to come back. Liverpool gets a bagging but I was so proud of the place. Bill was like a kid in a candy shop. He thought you just walked around Liverpool and bumped into ex-players! It is a funny thing in Liverpool that players can walk down the road and not get hassled. Jimmy was great."

Leo Byrne from Tralee in Ireland made his first visit to Anfield in the early 1990s – and not on a match day either. He arrived at the ground to find some first team players such as Paul Stewart and Steve Nicol who had finished training. He spoke to the players and got some autographs. That's how it used to be. These days the players are rarely seen at Anfield, except on match days of course, and it has always been tougher to gain access to them at Melwood where they come and go through security gates in their top of the range cars. In the 1970s I was one of a number of school kids who occasionally hung around Melwood trying to get a glimpse of the players or an autograph. Joey Jones, the Welsh international and a Kop favourite, was always the most approachable in that era when we would shove scraps of paper and a pen through the window of the coach and hope to get a player's signature.

Even then, not all players shared Jones' willingness to "give something back to the fans" and the general feeling among supporters is that a chasm has grown between the people in the stands and those on the field in the 30-odd years since. Even when players do stop for a minute to mingle with supporters they may not maintain eye contact or may have headphones playing music to distract them from the ordeal of mixing with the great unwashed. When you look at some fans' pictures taken on mobile phones with players you can almost see the reluctance in the eyes of the star who appears to be moving away even as the shutter captures the image. This is not directed at Liverpool specifically and anyway there a number of reasons why "the talent" and the fans exist in different worlds. Money obviously, demands on players' time, reluctance to sign merchandise that could later be sold on ebay, even language or cultural differences as a result of more international players coming into the game. Up to 1990 only 17 players in the history of the club had been born outside Britain and Ireland (north and south), but in the last two decades there have been players from all over the world on the books. Some of the foreign players formed strong attachments with the fans, anyway. Jan Molby, Didi Hamann, Sami Hyypia and Xabi Alonso achieved honorary Scouser status and in the current team Pepe Reina seems firmly established as "one of us" while Dirk Kuyt always appears to be good at mixing with the fans.

Of course, a player's nationality or his personality doesn't determine his popularity. What matters most is can he play or not? Liverpool's most popular players in any fans' poll will be on there because they have been successful as we can see if we look at those who are widely acknowledged as being the number one stars from each of the past six decades. Let's accept that these idols or Anfield A-listers are Billy Liddell in the 1950s, Roger Hunt (1960s), Kenny Dalglish (1970s and 1980s), Robbie Fowler (1990s), and Steven Gerrard ('Noughties'). (Dalglish spans two decades but, as he is widely acknowledged as the greatest ever Liverpool player, he deserves to be king of two decades). Interestingly, two of the five are Scots who settled in the Merseyside area (Liddell was a justice of the peace in the city and a bursar at the university), two are Scousers and Hunt was born less than 20 miles from Anfield, in Golborne near Wigan, making him, without doubt, the greatest "woollyback" to play for Liverpool. Only Fowler's inclusion could be debated. If we forget what we know now about that move to Manchester United, we could say that Michael Owen has a claim to be considered player of the 1990s. After all, he and Fowler both burst on to the scene then and their goal scoring records for Liverpool are similar (183 for Fowler compared to 158 for Owen, who played fewer games for the Reds). Owen, who made his debut in 1998, single handedly won an FA Cup for Liverpool with two goals in the 2001 final. Fowler failed to get on the score sheet in the 1996 FA Cup final or the League Cup final of 1995, but his only other rival in terms of football excellence at Liverpool in the 1990s was his good friend, Steve McManaman. But when it came to a popularity poll between McManaman and Fowler, the former would be the first to admit that there was never any contest. Fowler had grass roots support on the Kop and remains a player much respected by Liverpudlians.

Liddell and Gerrard were both considered to be effectively one-man teams for Liverpool. Liddell scored 228 goals in 534 matches for his club and it was his bad luck that he was born in the 1920s and so was too old to benefit from Bill Shankly's management. We were known as "Liddellpool" in the 1950s and if you look at the record books you can see why. Similar claims were made about Gerrard's influence, but even allowing for massive changes in the game, Liverpool are a much better team these days than they were when Liddell was around.

Looking at all our five heroes from decades past, there are two clear reasons why they were <u>the</u> stars of the decade as far as the fans were concerned – matches played and goals scored. In total, these five players made well over 2,000 appearances between them and scored more than 1,000 goals before the start of the 2010-11 season. So for all wannabe future Liverpool all-time greats all you need to do is play about 500 first team games and score about 200 goals and then we will love you forever. Easy as that.

Even those whose achievements are not as stellar find that Liverpool never really leaves them. Once the fans like you at our club, if you play your cards right, you are welcome back for life. Gary McAllister is a case in point. He was 35 when he joined Liverpool and has the dubious honour of being the final player to be older than me to play for the club while I watched him from the stands. For that reason I was always a big Gary Mac fan, but then he also had the good sense to score a free kick from 40-yards to win a Merseyside derby, earning him all-time hero status in an instant. In fact, McAllister played fewer than 90 matches for Liverpool and yet he is firmly associated with the club in a way that Larry Lloyd, Stan Collymore or even Jamie Redknapp never can be. It wasn't just McAllister's performances on the pitch, we also liked the way he remained supportive towards LFC after his departure and never criticised the club in public, unlike the players listed above.

Liverpool fans like to consider themselves fair minded but occasionally players will get stick from the crowd. Often the key target is a central midfielder such as Danny Murphy or Lucas Leiva who may be accused of slowing the tempo down too much or giving the ball away too often. Even Ronnie Whelan, who was a key man in the great teams of the 1980s, had to put up with criticism which was over the top.

In some cases the opposite is true and players get more than their fair share of praise. Neil "Razor" Ruddock was popular with Kopites who used to chant his name when he was a regular under Graeme Souness and Roy Evans in the 1990s. But Ruddock seemed to live a charmed life and was able to cultivate a loveable rogue image despite a lack of fitness and an unprofessional attitude on and off the pitch. Ruddock, who could hit a mean cross field pass when he put his mind to it, was seen by some as a swashbuckling figure who secured his legacy by scoring the equaliser in a dramatic match against Manchester United when we had been 3-0 down. To others he was a bluffer who never seemed to belong in the Liverpool red despite playing more than 150 times for us.

Ruddock just happened to be around in what became known as the Spice Boys era. I remember in 1995 seeing a crowd of young ladies outside the Main Stand at Anfield. They knew that pop star Robbie Williams, who was in the last throes of Take That first time round, had been at the match and was just about to head out in his ankle length look-at-me fur coat. It was a snapshot from a celebrity obsessed time when too many Liverpool players became besotted with the trappings of Premier League football and neglected the basics.

Gerard Houllier, who helped raise standards and impose discipline at Liverpool in his first three years as manager before ill-health and poor judgment tarnished his reputation, was aware that the relationship between players, media and fans could make his job a whole lot harder. Houllier remarked that there was an army of ex-Liverpool players in the press box every time his side played and he suggested these pundits were a hindrance. A bitter feud developed between Houllier and Ian St John which poisoned the atmosphere.

Other old pros have preferred to be part of the inner circle, earning money in the corporate hospitality and meet and greet business. Ex-players such as David Johnson, Phil Neal and Alan Kennedy are regulars in the executive boxes and function rooms at Anfield, regaling Liverpool's prawn sandwich brigade with tales from LFC's more successful times. Others, such as Molby and Tommy Smith, have also done their bit on the after dinner speaking circuit. Stories of Paisley, Dalglish and most of all Shankly will always be of interest to Liverpool fans of a certain age, no matter how many times we have heard them before.

One of the main complaints from Liverpool fans in Asia during the 2009 summer tour was that they could not get as much access to the players as they wanted. Sometimes it is hard to know whether the fault lies with the players for shutting themselves away or with the club's support team, agents and other assorted hangers-on for keeping supporters at arm's length.

Many of the jaded types of my age appreciate that these days, more than ever, we cheer the shirt rather than individual players. When Craig Bellamy scored goals for Liverpool I applauded like everyone else, although I didn't care for his public image. Ditto Collymore. In 2002, I was delighted when Lee Bowyer's move to Anfield fell through as I would have found it unpalatable to get behind a player with his off-the-field track record. Be under no illusions, some of the 700 players who played for Liverpool over the years you would not have wanted to meet socially.

Each time I leave home to go to Anfield, my wife Lucia has her own favourite comment. "Your dad's off to watch a bunch of millionaires have a kick about in the park," she tells the kids. She's dead right, of course and I am one of the mug punters who has helped make these characters what they are today with my match tickets and Sky subscriptions. But when it comes to supporting Liverpool's favourite central defender and his charity, the cost is somehow much easier to bear.

13.

A history of violence

"You'll never reach the station." **Chant sung to visiting supporters at Anfield, circa 1977**

The date is April 17, 1985, and the time is about 10pm after an FA Cup semi-final replay on a mild Wednesday night in Manchester. From my place in the Kippax terrace at Maine Road, I watch a group of Manchester United fans, whose team has just come from behind to win 2-1, run on to the pitch to taunt us. Mounted police officers react quickly to prevent serious clashes. Liverpool fans around me are in an ugly mood as we file out of the ground. Out of the pack, one of the young men takes out his rage by throwing something through the ground floor window of a terraced house. This is the signal for a mob to run up the road in Moss Side and attack parked cars. Some of the men attempt to overturn a car.

To the sounds of police sirens, groups of fans board Greater Manchester double-decker buses. But the mood of the passengers is just as violent as it had been on the streets. As the fans head into Manchester City Centre, the Liverpool mob sees their rivals walking in groups.

Fans wrench a metal handrail from the bus, open the emergency exits and hurl a makeshift spear as the vehicle continues to motor on at 40 miles per hour.

Finally, the bus arrives at Victoria Station. The driver avoids eye contact, opens the doors and lets the remainder of the scene play itself out, relieved he has done his job and is still in one piece, even if his bus isn't. As each fan gets off, he (it's all blokes) is greeted by a truncheon around the shoulder administered by an officer who has long since given up on thoughts of fair play. There is an almost ritual feel about the assaults which happen quickly and brutally. But I get lucky. There is an incident elsewhere and the police get distracted. I run off the bus in the confusion, avoiding the truncheon, and for me the night passes without further incident.

For about six weeks, until Heysel, these were some of the worst scenes I had seen at or outside a football match. In fact, in terms of sheer naked hatred, the Manchester United v Liverpool FA Cup semi-final replay at Maine Road all those years ago takes some beating (forgive the pun). In the years since I look back on that night with a shudder and remember that, as bad as it was, it might have been even worse. To some, such scenes a quarter of a century on may seem shocking and the problems above were hardly typical of your average match day. Around this time, we stood on the Kop many times and saw no problems and felt no threat.

What's even stranger about that game at Maine Road is its ordinariness to many of the fans who were there and were following football in those days. Liverpool supporters such as Nicky Allt and Tony Evans who have written books about following the team in the 1980s, mention the FA Cup semi-final replay and I think both were in the same section as I was and yet they only refer to it in passing. In fact Evans, who is now football editor for *The Times* and travelled to far more away games than I did, writes in his book *Far Foreign Land* the match passed "without trouble". Evans understandably suggests that the problems at the first semi-final match in 1985 when Liverpool and United drew 2-2 were much worse. In the first game rival fans threw golf balls with nails embedded in them and flares at each other in a notorious meeting at Goodison Park. For a time in the 1980s, football violence appeared out of control and a collective madness would descend whenever United and Liverpool played each other.

Thankfully, football has moved on and several years ago when journalist Chris Bascombe wrote that problems between United and Liverpool had reached a "new low" I had to disagree. Violence was a fact of life for the higher risk fixtures between 1970 and the late 1980s and there are some well documented cases on both sides of fans bearing the brunt. Poisonous may still be a valid word to describe the atmosphere of that game, but that is progress of sorts compared to an era of tear gas attacks and fans on both sides being stabbed and slashed. Another personal example was at Old Trafford about 1984 when I was fortunate enough to duck just as a pool ball went whizzing past my head and hit a wall behind me in the Scoreboard End.

Memories of these violent days were in my mind in 2007 when there was the prospect of Liverpool and Manchester United meeting in the Champions League final in Athens. There were enough problems in Greece as it was, but had it been Liverpool v United rather than

Milan who knows what might have happened. Times may have changed, many of the older lads who used to cause trouble may have moved on and grown up and policing may have become more sophisticated, but the threat remains.

One man who is well qualified to comment on this is David Wilson, who is that rare breed, a Liverpool supporter living in Manchester. He runs a branch of Mancs who have seen the light and prefer a Liverbird to a Red Devil on their shirt. He traces the problems of the last few decades to a match at Old Trafford in the late 1960s when Liverpool supporters "took" the Stretford End. For the benefit of younger readers used to all-seater stadiums and segregated crowds, "taking" ends was once a common feature of football hooliganism. It was an act of bravado which resulted in a lot of running, swinging police truncheons and much fear among innocent fans.

For Liverpool-born Wilson, what should have been a happy memory turned into a violent and troubling experience in enemy territory. He says: "In 1990, the Mancs were rebuilding Old Trafford and they only gave Liverpool 60 tickets. I was in the United end and I managed to keep a low profile at first, even when we scored. But then Ian Rush made it 2-0 and I could not control myself. There was a lot of things said when I was in the ground but after the game I got twatted. The police knew what happened but they said it was my own fault."

And it wasn't just in and around the ground that problems could arise, as Wilson recalls. "A guy put an ad in the *Manchester Evening News* saying 'if there are any Liverpool fans who want to join the supporters club, ring me'. He had his car smashed and his house was vandalised. When I formed this Liverpool supporters' club I was advised to keep a low profile, which I do. I have had a few phone calls from dickhead Man United fans. I got some on a Saturday when they won the Premiership. I had a phone call at 3.30am – the language was awful."

But who is to say that Manchester United fans don't have their own horror stories as a result of run-ins with Liverpool supporters? And, as Wilson happily acknowledges, he has enjoyed a lot of healthy and good natured banter with United fans, even after United missed out on a place at the 2007 Champions League final. The big Internet joke at the time was that United's sponsors were AIG (Almost in Greece). Dave was only too pleased to pass this email on to colleagues.

It is hard to pin down the whens and whys of football hooliganism. It is often seen as a modern curse, but history books show there were problems in grounds before the First World War and in the 1950s there was a spate of train wrecking on the notorious soccer specials. But from the late 1960s with the growth of skinhead fashion and more fans being able to travel by road and rail, there were more opportunities for hooligans to get their weekly fix of trouble. In his book *Anfield of Dreams,* Neil Dunkin recalls seeing his first case of football related violence at a Chelsea v Liverpool match at Stamford Bridge in the early 1960s. In 1966 there were serious incidents at the Liverpool v Celtic Cup Winners' Cup semi-final at Anfield. Celtic fans infamously threw bottles on to the pitch and forced the match to be stopped for a time. My dad, for reasons he still can't explain, was standing in the Anfield Road End that night as the whisky bottles flew over his head. Afterwards, Bill Shankly asked his friend

Jock Stein, the Celtic manager "Jock, do you want your share of the gate money or shall we just return the empties?"

By 1971, Manchester United were being plagued by regular crowd trouble and at the start of the 1971-72 season they were forced to play a "home" match against Arsenal at, of all places, Anfield. This was a result of Old Trafford being closed after knives were thrown into the away section at the end of the previous season. As Greg Roughley reported in *The Guardian* online in March 2010, United players from that time conveniently deny any knowledge of ever having to play a home match at Anfield. But Roughley has the match programme complete with picture of Shanks on the front, as evidence.

It is sad but true to say that on many occasions between 1970 and 1990, aggro at the match was a fact of life. Liverpool's 7-0 win against Tottenham in 1978 is remembered for a superb team performance rounded off by Terry McDermott's header, but I also recall being 12 at the time and seeing a Tottenham fan wearing a replica shirt being set upon by a group of hooligans near the entrance to Stanley Park. My dad told the police, but it was a sign of the times that in those days fans would no doubt criticise the Spurs fans for being foolish in wearing colours at an away match.

Back then, the rowdy element was more likely to stand in the Anfield Road End than the Kop and it shows how much times have changed that these days some of those lads are raconteurs with their own shows at Liverpool's theatres while the deadly Road End of yore is now tourist central on match days and you are more likely to get your eye taken out by the point of a jester's hat than a dart.

The authorities have largely managed hooliganism out of the game by the use of police intelligence, CCTV and banning orders. Crowd trouble has never fully disappeared from English football, although it is now a fringe rather than a mainstream issue. Police officers talk of "risk supporters" who may be as few as 150 out of a crowd of 60,000. These bad 'uns have to be watched and there is still potential for matters to turn nasty in certain high risk fixtures.

But the match day atmosphere at Anfield has changed dramatically and fans who once chanted "Ten Past Nine is stabbing time", "We'll see you all outside" and "You'll never reach the station" to away fans have long since had to clean up their act. There is a lot to regret about the changes in football, but the prospects of getting your head kicked in have been significantly reduced. It is now rare to see trouble, certainly at Anfield. But to get to this point, we can't overlook hooliganism's bleakest moment and Liverpool's role in it.

Heysel – football's tragic acid trip

Heysel was tragic and bizarre at the same time. Like many others who have written about that night in Brussels a quarter of a century on, I find it difficult to believe I saw some of the things that went on, even before the horror of the wall collapsing. There were police officers confiscating flag poles and then leaving them for queues of supporters behind them to trip over; the crumbling ground; the lack of ticket checks; the chicken fence which separated the Liverpool fans from the "neutral" areas of Area Z where 39 supporters died. Later, I still wonder if I really did see a teenage Liverpool fan make several attempts to grab a weapon from the holster of a Belgian policeman during the height of the disorder. Then there were the two hours of rioting from the Juventus fans, the Italian brandishing a "starter pistol", the Liverpool supporter being chased by packs of Juve supporters and being hit by a brick. There was also the fact that the match even went ahead and finally the fires that were burning symbolically on a hellish night as we left the ground. I saw it all — the chaos, the charge from several hundred Liverpool fans and the aftermath. I saw it, but didn't register what had happened at the time. In these days of mobile phones and news going around the world quicker than ever, it may be hard to believe but it wasn't until after the match that we found out that people had died.

In his book, *From Where I Was Standing* Liverpool fan Chris Rowland suggests that hooliganism was one crucial reason for the Heysel tragedy, but not the only one. He wrote:

> "The deaths...were wholly preventable. They were the obscene consequences of gross negligence, stupefying incompetence, criminal lack of forethought and a whole succession of people... failing to do their jobs properly. The violence on the terraces was the tipping point and the unfit ground, inept policing and terror of the retreating Juventus fans led to the carnage on a warm spring evening."

The journalist Brian Reade wrote a play based on his experiences on the disaster in which a young Liverpool supporter was forced to come to terms with his role. "It read like someone explaining their first bad acid trip," Reade recalled in his excellent LFC memoir *44 Years*

With the Same Bird. Heysel has also inspired – if that's the right word – a fictional account *In the Crowd* by Laurent Mauviginer. This novel tells the story of Heysel through the eyes of fans from different parts of Europe and a key character is Geoff Andrewson, a Scouser who goes to Belgium with his beery, brawling brothers. In an evocative ending, Andrewson takes stock both of the culture of football violence and his life on Merseyside and asks if he was to blame. Twenty-five years on it still makes for uncomfortable reading.

Each year it becomes more difficult to untangle myth and reality from the bitter legacy of Heysel. Rival fans who chant "murderers" at Liverpool supporters made up their minds long ago about who was to blame. Do those rival fans know or care about the ticketing fiasco, the selection of an inadequate ground in the first place or the role of the Belgian police? I first heard Everton fans shout "killers" at Liverpool fans at Goodison in 1985 during Kenny Dalglish's first Merseyside derby as player-manager. At least Everton's taunts can be seen in light of their historic resentment at being denied a chance to play in the European Cup in 1985. Manchester United's followers seem to use the "murderers" tag just to wind up their rivals from the other side of the East Lancs Road. When United fans were attacked by riot police in Rome in 2007, the feeling from Liverpool supporters was not that the Mancs had got a good hiding but depression that the potential for another Heysel still exists in parts of Europe.

Hours after the rioting at Heysel, my mate and I slept rough at Brussels station, wondering if we would get back home in one piece. We later met a *Liverpool Echo* journalist and my comments were reported in the paper the following day. I hadn't seen them for 25 years until I researched this book. "The organisation was abysmal," I was accurately quoted as saying in the article, backing up eyewitness accounts of thousands of other Reds. In the years since, some have claimed that Liverpool fans have denied responsibility for Heysel, that they have been guilty of blame shifting. It isn't credible just to suggest, as some have done, that Liverpool fans were simply caught up in bother and the rest was a tragic mistake. Claims – which probably have some credence – that right wing agent groups were active in Belgium back then may be part of the story but this has never been categorically determined. As for the well known accusation that a young Liverpool fan was being attacked by Juventus fans shortly before the charge, I never saw this and just don't know if it provoked the fatal violence or not.

We may not like to admit it but numbers of Liverpool fans were causing problems in the hours before the catastrophic scenes in the ground. There were disturbances in the city centre long before kick-off and that's why many of us were keen to get to the ground in plenty of time. In the fields around Heysel I saw groups of fans in a drunken and antisocial mood. There was an undercurrent of tension throughout the late afternoon and early evening. Later on, the hair trigger tempers snapped and we saw the fans breaking through the barriers and charging at the Italian fans.

Some – possibly several hundred – were involved in the incidents to some extent. I wasn't. But I knew as I stood there in that ground with the steps literally crumbling under my feet that I wouldn't be seeing Liverpool play in Europe any time soon. But for others, the 1985 European Cup final, left a much deeper, tragic legacy.

Sadly, hooliganism was a serious problem even before the nadir of Belgium. Nineteen eighty-four/eighty-five was a bad season for fans who wanted to stay out of trouble. I saw incidents of all kinds that season – running battles against Sheffield Wednesday, fans being slashed at Chelsea in the autumn, isolated incidents at Barnsley in the FA Cup in February 1985 and then the two brutal semi-finals with Manchester United in April. There were also many outbreaks of violence that didn't involve Liverpool around this time. There was the Luton/Millwall riot and the death of a 14-year-old boy at Birmingham City on the last day of the league season on the same day as the Bradford fire, which like Hillsborough, had nothing to do with hooliganism, claimed 56 lives.

In 1985 football was hit by a perfect storm of violence from the fans and incompetence from its administrators. To mark the 25th anniversary of the Heysel disaster, the *Liverpool Echo* interviewed Peter Robinson, who was Liverpool FC's secretary at the time. It was well known that Robinson had warned anyone who would listen just how serious the prospects were of something going wrong in Brussels. What isn't well known is that his messages and telexes were simply ignored by the police and UEFA who said that they had everything under control.

We have to understand that background of negligence to make any sense of Heysel. Let's accept that hundreds of Liverpool fans were in the wrong. Now let's also accept that UEFA chose a decrepit ground, allowed segregation to break down and arrogantly ignored advice, pleadings even, from Liverpool FC weeks before the game to take urgent action. Let's also accept that the Belgian police were ineffectual. Finally, let's say Juventus fans at the other end, the Drughi, were hardly blameless. Their role in Heysel has often been glossed over because it is an inconvenient part of the terrible story. It makes a straightforward English hooligan issue just too complicated for some. Were Juve's fans enraged by what had happened at the other end of the ground? And if they did know, did this excuse their missile throwing and pitch invasions which led to the mounted police finally moving in? And, as others have pointed out before me, the infamous 'Reds Animals' banner unveiled at the opposite end to where we were, showed provocation was on the agenda for some long before the trouble. And yet none of this could or should excuse what happened.

Other memories of Heysel stay in the mind, one of which is Joe Fagan, in his last game as Liverpool manager. He was in tears as he walked towards the terraces to appeal for peace. The tears were of emotion, frustration and also shock at the way the game he loved so much had gone so terribly wrong. Later, on the boat back to England, there was only one topic of conversation. I remember a fan suggesting that he was glad that Shanks hadn't lived to see his beloved club in the gutter. Others openly suggested they were finished with football.

Heysel remains a scar on Liverpool's history. When Juventus played at Anfield in the Champions League 20 years after the disaster in 2005, there were ceremonies to honour the dead. Some of the visiting Italians turned their backs in a sign that they weren't prepared to accept any apologies. Five years later, Phil Neal, who was captain on the night of the Heysel game and tried in vain to appeal for calm over the PA, helped unveil a plaque at Anfield outside the Centenary Stand which remembers the victims of the disaster. Football matches were organised between people from the two cities in the months after the disaster and again in 2010.

Heysel marked the stage when Liverpool fans had to re-assess the whole basis of their support for their club. The press reported that it was "the night football died" and for a while that looked to be correct. Liverpool supporters had to, and still must, take responsibility for what happened.

14.

Torn in the USA

"Tom Hicks and George Gillett, just by being born in America, have made it that much harder for Americans to follow a club they love." **OhYouBeauty Blog**

On the day Rafa Benitez's departure from Liverpool was announced, there were demonstrations around Anfield. A small group of fans, protesting against Liverpool's owners, set fire to an American flag. It made for vivid pictures in the next day's papers and some shaking of heads on both sides of the Atlantic. On the Liverpool Echo's online message board, a number of Merseyside based supporters deplored the action, saying it had condemned a nation of almost 300million because of the actions of two men. In the 1960s and early 1970s, radical Americans burned the stars and stripes flags in protest against the Vietnam War as a matter of routine. But that was during an era of deep social divisions in the States and since 9/11 everyone from the president to the doorman at a hotel feels obliged to wear the nation's emblem proudly on their suit lapel to show solidarity with those who died in the atrocities.

The port of Liverpool was historically the gateway to the new world for people and goods. Liverpool's economic wealth in the 19th Century was largely due to its trade with the United States. It is a grim fact that the slave trade was a major factor in Liverpool providing so much wealth for so few. A hundred years later, the cultural influences of America were a vital influence on The Beatles who grew up loving US Rock and Roll in the 1950s.

Many of these historical connections are meaningful to fans in the nine affiliated supporters' branches across the United States. If Hicks and Gillett's names were mud in Liverpool in 2010 they were hardly popular in their homeland either. You could almost hear the exasperation coming through the keyboards when a 27-year-old US blogger and Liverpool fan called Nate, posted on his site *OhYouBeauty* in June 2010: "The last thing we need right now is division amongst honest-to-goodness supporters. Everyone needs to be focused on removing Hicks and Gillett, and it's not because of their nationality."

Nate's post attracted a strong response and one fan, Jason B, wrote: "There's no excuse. It (the flag burning) was a shameful display and I'm embarrassed to be a Liverpool fan after seeing it. Our dislike of Hicks and Gillette (sic) doesn't make it OK. It's out of bounds and it's out of line."

Two months before the flag burning, in a separate online interview with *just-football.com*, Nate said: "It's hard commenting on this as an American, because it feels as if you're automatically grouped in with your countrymen, but the solution's simple – Gillett and Hicks have to go. They've damaged the club's financial situation, hopefully not irreparably, lied about the debt, and failed to fund any transfers outside of what Rafa's recouped for three windows now. On the other side of the ocean, I honestly wish I had more knowledge of, and involvement in, Spirit of Shankly, but as far as I can tell, they're doing God's work."

I have to confess that America provided me with some of the biggest surprises in the research of this book. It is an extraordinary place and as Liverpool fans we should be proud of the backing we get there. Don't believe me? Then read on.

There once was a rent-a-gob Chelsea fan called Steven Cohen who was a pundit on George W. Bush's favourite TV channel, Fox. By all accounts, Cohen had cheesed off Liverpool's big Stateside following for some time with his "provocative" comments. But in April 2009, on the same week as 20th anniversary of the Hillsborough tragedy, Cohen took one swim too many in the media sewer. In a Kelvin McKenzie-esque rant he blamed Liverpool supporters for the deaths of 96 fans in Sheffield. This might have been dismissed as just another offensive outburst by a blowhard – but then something wonderful happened. A campaign, brilliant in its conception and execution, began in New York. The fans informed Cohen of the error of his ways and he responded with a toe curling non-apology-apology in which he cited freedom of speech, mom's apple pie and used the unconvincing stock response of all extremists when they are backed into a corner: "I have received death threats."

But the New Yorkers were far too angry and far too clever to form a lynch mob. They knew that was just what Cohen wanted and instead did what any savvy

American activist would do – they went for the wallet. Targeting advertisers, the campaigners threatened to boycott all products which advertised on Fox. Sports bars, magazines and merchandisers were all involved. Steve Nicol, coach of the Major League Soccer team New England Revolution and a member of the Liverpool team that day at Hillsborough, ended contact with Cohen. Liverpool FC came out strongly against Cohen and Chelsea stated they had nothing to do with him and would not disrespect the memories of the 96. And after all the emails, the campaigning and all the pressure, it worked. Cohen was thrown off air and replaced by ex-US football international Eric Wynalda.

Daragh Kennedy, the Irish born president of the New York Supporters' branch, said: "It was an incredible effort. Our outgoing vice president Conor Brennan was the one who orchestrated the whole thing. He is involved with the media and he edits our podcast. He – like all of us – was outraged by Cohen's comments which go back some years. He (Cohen) said things, apologised and retracted statements and said he wouldn't say them again. We felt enough was enough. A lot of members felt very passionate about it and we decided to do something about it. We did target the advertisers; a lot of them were American companies who maybe didn't understand the connotations of what happened. We set out on a campaign to educate those advertisers and we had our members contact the advertisers to let them know how they felt. It took on a life of its own. Other supporters' clubs in America got involved and we had a lot of support in England.

"It was David versus Goliath and you wouldn't think a bunch of football fans could have that clout, but Conor ran an incredible campaign – the amount of energy he put into it…Once the advertisers were made aware of what transpired and what was said, they were on edge. The emails were continuous and then the advertisers thought 'we are trying to reach out to a small community and we don't want to offend them.' People were outraged; people who knew about what happened and a few of the branch members had been at the game. I remember watching it myself. I just think there was a feeling of us against them and that no-one was going to rest until we got the desired result."

Kennedy, a son of Dublin, went to New York 20 years ago and despite remaining a proud Irishman, has assimilated into the American way of life. He jokes that one day he will start a timesheet on all the hours he spends on supporters' club business. In July, August and September that could amount to 30 hours a week on top of a full time job. "My dedication comes from a sense of organisation. I feel that if you are going to do something, do it right and I don't believe in doing things half-arsed. If you go back to the beginning, the (supporters') club was predominantly made up of Irish and English immigrants and there was a sense of community and friendship. As the years have gone on we have got away from that as Irish people have gone home. Our club is now 50-70% American and the majority have come on board since Istanbul. We have tried to regain the community spirit by doing things as a club – quizzes, community events, charity events with the New York Red Bulls MLS team. In 2004, we went up to Connecticut when Liverpool played in a pre-season game. We are trying to be everything to everybody, but some people just want to come to the bar and have a few drinks. Some people want tickets for the matches and when you try to cater to everyone's tastes there will be people who think we are trying to do too much."

New York is always a popular destination for ex-Liverpool players who hold "an evening with" events. Ex-Reds Phil Neal, Ian Callaghan and Jimmy Melia have all had speaking engagements in the city, but big Jan Molby was Kennedy's favourite guest. "An absolutely classic player and a class man. I can't say enough good things about him. It was just like sitting down with one of my mates. When he came over it was one of the best days of my presidency of the club and certainly as a Liverpool fan it was a very big highlight."

In the US, fans who have supported Liverpool since the 1980s and earlier are not always keen on the Johnny Come Latelys. Kennedy said: "Some think that Americans are jumping on the bandwagon since Istanbul and they are not real fans, but I don't have that view. I think anyone who wants to be a Liverpool fan is welcome and we all started off sometime."

No one could accuse Connie Lofton of being a casual Liverpool fan. In fact she jokingly describes herself as one of the "auld arses" of the New York contingent. So why did she first become a Red? "The two players who really grabbed my attention in the matches I saw were Robbie Fowler and Steve McManaman. Also, one of the sports channels around that time actually showed a weekly roundup of league goals – I saw John Barnes on more than one occasion and thought he was the bee's knees. Also a mad Liverpool-supporting friend from Ireland was living here at that time, so I picked up interest/knowledge from her. The interest in Liverpool in particular has usually spiked after a successful season (as you'd expect) – tons of new supporters after Istanbul of course but there was a decent spike after the FA Cup win in 2006 as well."

For Lofton, like so many other Liverpool fans abroad, watching their team is a key part of their social life. "It's the camaraderie – end of. You see the same faces week in/week out, which is nice. And while I personally have always had a group of folks over the years that I drank/discussed the match with, there's a good group of 10-15 of us that have really bonded over the last three or four seasons that I can't imagine spending the weekend without. We watched the World Cup this summer as well, as we did the European Championships two years ago."

Another of the New York branch members who pays his $20 a season subs is Liverpool-born journalist Jim Edwards. He watches Liverpool matches with his mates in the 11th Street bar in Manhattan. "The Americans are often new to the cause and the interesting thing is the Americans are more enthusiastic than many of the English fans. They have the zeal of the newly converted. As soon as they get into Liverpool they want to know everything – all the history, the songs and they quickly book their flights to go over to Anfield twice a year. They end up knowing more than I do."

So why Liverpool? Edwards said: "My latest theory was picked up by going to the Maritime Museum at Albert Dock. There is a whole exhibition there about how a lot of Liverpudlians got on a boat and emigrated to New York at the beginning of the last century. Liverpool and New York have a very long and historic connection and a lot of people think parts of the cities are very similar. Also there is a lot of support for Liverpool through the club's links with Ireland. The Irish moved to New York en masse in the 1990s – in hundreds of thousands – and many stayed. Why do Americans who have never been to England support Liverpool? I have asked them this and the story is always the same. 'I was just randomly flicking through the channels for something to watch and I saw this Liverpool game. I carried on watching and by the end I was addicted.'"

About 200 miles away on the East coast, the Phoenix Landing bar on the main drag in Cambridge, Massachusetts is home to the LFC Boston Branch. Cambridge, which is known to Britons as the home of Harvard University, is also a favourite meeting place for a dedicated group of Liverpool fans. Their pub of choice is typically Irish in design – like many places in the Boston area – and you can find shamrocks and a decent pint of Guinness. But unlike most American sports bars where the action seems to be just moving wallpaper, in this place football really matters. That's largely due to the efforts of a hard working group of supporters, most of whom were bitten by the Liverpool bug when one Michael Owen was in his pomp. He is unlikely to be forgiven for his move to the wrong side of the East Lancs Road, but Owen's historic goal for England against Argentina in the 1998 World Cup was a landmark event for many in the US. It seems to have stirred support for Liverpool which remains strong to this day.

"When Liverpool played Man United at 7am there were 100 people lining up outside the door," said Ethan Armstrong, one of the Bostonian fans. "In the World Cup of 2006 I was in a pub called the Coat of Arms in

New Hampshire. England were playing Sweden and I just remember the atmosphere. I also remember seeing Peter Crouch and thinking 'who the hell is this guy?' He looked more like a basketball player. It started from there, but I really felt like a Liverpool fan when Newcastle beat us over Christmas a few years ago – I was devastated. That's when I realised I was a fan – I felt crushed. In the US we don't have cup competitions or anything like the Champions League so at first I didn't understand what Istanbul meant. It is only now that I know more about Liverpool's history that I can see the importance of the Champions League and the FA Cup."

Sarah Keddy lives in New England but gained a love for the Reds in old England where she spent nine months in college in London. She said: "Liverpool does seem to be the team that has the strongest community base in this country. We have links with fans with fans in New York and we all have a common purpose."

Steve Nicol, who has had a successful coaching career with the New England Revolution, believes American football has a lot to offer, but in an email interview for this book, said that interest in the game's original stronghold remains on a much bigger scale. "It's just the culture… it's different. In Britain, every living breathing person knows about football – soccer, whatever you want to call it – and has some interest in it in some capacity, whereas here it's just not a culture yet. Most people here just associate you with Liverpool, so whatever's happening that day is relevant to you. People don't see me as an ex-Liverpool player here. When Liverpool play and win, people congratulate me. I don't know why, it's been 15 years since I was there. But I guess they see that if you're part of something, you're always going to be part of it, whereas in Britain, people tend to look at you as an ex-something."

Before Hicks and Gillett entered our world, America's influence over Liverpool was notable mainly for an after dinner anecdote about Bill Shankly who reputedly refused to put his watch back when on a tour in the States and kept to UK time. Shanks was also bewildered that the Americans didn't share his obsession with football and he couldn't believe that "they haven't heard of Tom Finney". Later, we had the short and not so successful goalkeeping stint of Brad Friedel, who moved to Anfield from Columbus Crew but built his reputation later at Blackburn and Aston Villa.

These days it's all about money. Like Asia, America is seen as a potential growth area for Liverpool FC, the business. There are a dozen affiliated branches in North America (three of them in Canada) and in 2009 the club signed an extended four-year £5million sponsorship deal with Bank of America. The deal covers a range of agreements including enabling the bank to use the LFC logo and gain access to corporate seats.

But it's the mountain of money owed to the banks rather than the sums coming in that leaves the American Liverpool supporters feeling uneasy. It's not their fault that they happen to share a nationality with two characters who are the source of such anger and resentment. And I for one hope those Kopites who shout "Yanks Out" appreciate that on the other side of the Atlantic there are legions of genuine supporters who have a big emotional stake in the club.

15.

Material Uncertainty

"LFC is not a commodity and it is what the fans think that matters and if the fans don't like what you are doing they will protest and you will be kicked out." **Kriss Maguire, Liverpool fan, from Aigburth**

July 4, 2010, a clammy Sunday afternoon in Liverpool, and a crowd has gathered at the city's St George's Hall plateau. They have chosen this familiar spot to protest against LFC's American owners, Tom Hicks and George Gillett. The rally has been organised on July 4 in a symbolic move to declare the fans' 'independence' from Hicks and Gillett who have been widely condemned for burdening the club with a high level of debt and failing to make good on promises about building a new stadium and attracting financial investment. Hicks and Gillett had already been forced to announce they were looking to sell the club more than three months earlier and their mismanagement of LFC had left the fans fearful of what the future might bring.

Since it was built about 170 years ago, St George's Hall and the imposing plateau which stands proudly opposite Lime Street station, has been the backdrop for many a political protest. It was here in December 1980 that mourners paid their respects to murdered Beatle John Lennon and football fans have traditionally gathered at this focal point to salute triumphant Everton and Liverpool footballers on big occasions. In 2005 St George's Hall was thronged with fans celebrating the return from Istanbul. In 1971, Bill Shankly delivered an evocative call to arms for Liverpool supporters. With spellbinding oratory, Shanks addressed the fans who had gone into town to welcome the players back from their FA Cup final defeat by Arsenal. Claiming that China's Chairman Mao had never seen such a show of red strength, Shanks said that he always told his players that they were "privileged to play for you. If they didn't believe me before, they believe me now". Some reckon this was the moment when Liverpool's great team of the 1970s truly took shape and others reflected that had the manager told the fans to invade Birkenhead, they would have done so without question.

This speech is being played over the loud speaker 39 years later to a smaller but no less dedicated gathering. The independent Liverpool Supporters Union, the Spirit of Shankly, has organised the meeting and has attracted media attention and a range of speakers, comedians and musicians to provide entertainment to add some light relief to a day of protest. More than two years into its plan of action and opposition to the American regime, Spirit of Shankly is launching a community bank or credit union which, it is hoped, will enable fans the chance to pool finances and gain a share in the club they once thought was theirs. Spirit of Shankly announced it was in talks with Share Liverpool, an organisation formed by academic Rogan Taylor which was established for Liverpool fans to raise £5,000 each to buy a stake in LFC. That threshold was lowered to £500 as SOS announced plans to build a fighting fund. "We want our say and whether that is with 100% of the club or a smaller amount, we intend to have it," announce the leaflets handed out to those attending the free event.

Some who post messages on websites sneer and wonder how a relatively small group can mobilise genuine action against owners who are responsible for burdening Liverpool with a debt that could be anywhere between £300million and half a billion pounds. Fatalism and pessimism are understandable given Liverpool FC's plight.

But all fans I speak to are worried about the club's future and feel bruised by Hicks and Gillett's record. The pair are lampooned as Statler and Waldorf, those old American duffers who made smart Alec comments about their fellow Muppets in the 1970s. (The difference between the TV characters and the 2010 version is the original Statler and Waldorf made people laugh and confined their damage to the music hall).

Back to 2010 and on the stage at the summer event, trade union leader Billy Hayes and former Liverpool player John Aldridge spoke with passion about the need to change the way the club is run. Karen Gill, Shankly's granddaughter, reminded us how the man who made the people happy never believed in lost causes and would be reclaiming football for the people now if he was still with us. All stirring stuff, but the substance was provided by the organisers of Spirit of Shankly, the likes of Jay McKenna, a confident and articulate young media spokesperson, and Franny Stanton who said the July 4 meeting had been organised: "To show the people running Liverpool Football Club that no longer will we be treated with such contempt that they are showing to us at the moment. None of them have the best interests of Liverpool Football Club at heart. Tom Hicks and George Gillett want as much money as they can get so they can go back to their homes thousands of miles away. (Managing director) Christian Purslow and Martin Broughton (the LFC chairman) have the best interests of the banks who they work for their in their hearts. Everyone here today has the best interests of Liverpool Football Club at heart."

Down on the plateau, amid the burgers and banners, fans were keen to hear some good news after a barrage of damaging headlines. James Long, from Dovecot in Liverpool, said: "The club has always been a massive part of my life, so to see the downturn in the last couple of years is heartbreaking. We felt we should come down to show our support more than anything and to get more information on the Credit Union. Of all places it is right it should be here, the place Shankly spoke in 1971." But what kind of owners would he like to see take over? "It is easy to say 'the Man City style' where you throw money at it, but I don't know if that would fit in with Liverpool. Just as long as we have stability and are able to compete, I will be happy with that." And how optimistic was he that that would happen? "Not very. I think it will be a long, drawn-out process. Hopefully, events like today can push it along a bit and we can find the money from somewhere or find the money ourselves."

Kriss Maguire, from Aigburth, said: "This should send a message to any new owners that LFC is not a commodity and it is what the fans think that matters and if the fans don't like what you are doing they will protest and you will be kicked out. I don't know whether clubs like Chelsea or Manchester City are sustainable in the long term. You don't want a billionaire owner to throw money about and then leave because you won't be able to pay the players' wages and the club could go under. I like to be optimistic and hope we can get better owners. Anyone has to be better than these two we have now. Fingers crossed there will be some positive developments over the next few months."

So how did it all come to this? In many ways the chaotic story of Liverpool FC's ownership began in the 1990s. This was the decade when other clubs caught up and overtook Liverpool on and off the pitch. And all the time, the Premier League was demanding more and more. Soaring wage bills, huge costs for ground development, marketing and merchandising costs transformed the game. It came as shock for Liverpool whose lofty position in world football contrasted with a modest business model off it. The chairman and majority shareholder David Moores who was born into the Littlewoods business empire, did his best for many years. But by 1997 Liverpool FC were falling behind competitors who had increased ground capacity and had been smarter in maximising commercial revenue. Moores spent a long time looking for a suitable investor to pump money into Liverpool and recruited financial consultants to find the right buyer. Moores realised that Liverpool needed serious money to build a new stadium as well as attracting top name players who demanded rock star salaries. By the start of the new millennium Steve Morgan, who made his fortune in Redrow Housing and used to follow Liverpool from the Kop, wanted to get on the board but was seen as a predator by Moores who was not willing to co-operate. Then, the disgraced former Thai Prime Minister Thaksin Shinawatra was mentioned as a potential saviour but he became the first of Manchester City's unlikely sugar daddies.

Instead, Moores and his chief executive were left with a choice of selling Liverpool to Dubai Investment Capital or an American entrepreneur, George Gillett. DIC seemed to be a good option, but Moores was doubtful. He liked Gillett, felt he was a genuine guy with whom he could do business and, after apparently securing guarantees that Liverpool FC would be in good hands, asked his lawyers to do the deal.

Gillett had the vision and was plausible enough to Moores who could hardly be accused of selling Liverpool to the first person who came along. In fact, Moores' critics had accused him of dithering on the sale of the club during a tortuous process. No, it was time for him to listen to his instincts, to back his judgment and so Gillett it had to be. But there was to be one very significant and costly piece of small print. Gillett had a partner, someone Moores didn't know, a man who was seen as crucial to making the whole thing work. Tom Hicks was a straight talking Texan who could raise the money, bust some chops and give Anfield a business makeover courtesy of the USA. And so, in 2007, the press were summoned to Anfield and the good old boys waved scarves on the pitch and promised not to "do a Glazers" and load debt on to Liverpool FC. Moores was made life president, banked an estimated £88m and hoped his historic decision would lead to fresh ideas and an exciting new era for the club, including a superb new ground. A spade in the ground in two months, we were told.

There were warning signs even at that first media conference. With the benefit of hindsight, the Americans' plans seemed short on detail and a lot was taken on trust – a disastrous mistake by Moores and Parry as it later emerged. But when Hicks and Gillett described Liverpool as a magnificent franchise, we put that down to a trans-Atlantic language breakdown. Yes, we had doubts, but we were sure that Moores and his chief executive Rick Parry had negotiated guarantees. After all, the process of selling the club had been so longwinded and involved so many highly paid consultants, there was no way it could have been slapdash. Moores and Parry were genuine Reds after all. No way would they sell us down the Mersey. The world economy was still buoyant, the phrase 'credit crunch' had not been heard back in early 2007. What could go wrong?

Some embraced this time of change, some were doubtful and a small minority wisely declared at an early stage "this will all end in tears". Some reminded us that Moores has a poor record when it came to bringing people in as pairs. In the 1990s he appointed joint chief executives when Parry was recruited to work 'alongside' Peter Robinson and in 1998 he named Roy Evans and Gerard Houllier as joint managers. This just led to confusion, so why would joint owners be any different?

And yet, it all seemed to be going along well in the spring of 2007. The Americans did tend to disappear for long spells to re-emerge for the odd big match at Anfield or in an interview with a US or Canadian radio channel. But in those days they were returning calls from fans, logging on to message boards and generally listening. Gillett, in particular, seemed to care what we were saying. On the night Liverpool eliminated Barcelona in the Champions League, the pair had been seduced by the atmosphere and the history of their new club, we were assured. Then there was Athens and everything changed. There was a warning even before the Champions League final that the owners still had a lot to learn when they boasted about taking their families en masse to the match against AC Milan. This was an irritating statement to the thousands who weren't able to get tickets and it led to a chain of events which resulted in Rick Parry ruining his reputation among the majority of fans. But on the day after the 2-1 defeat to Milan there was a far more serious public statement. Rafa Benitez warned that money was required for transfers and told the owners bluntly that it was time to get the cheque book out. Hicks and Gillett – the Texan now had star billing – were on the back foot. In an attempt to calm fears, Hicks and Gillett sanctioned the purchase of Fernando Torres and Javier Mascherano. But the aftermath of Athens was notable for factionalism which at times later verged on internal civil war.

Athens was the first of a dizzying list of disputes. Rafa and the owners; Rafa and Hicks; Hicks and Parry; even Hicks and Gillett as the two famously had a bitter fall out and then refused to sit together on their rare outings to Merseyside. Rafa was given a public dressing down by Hicks and the owners sounded out Jurgen Klinsmann as a potential replacement as manager. Moreover, the Americans were not building the new stadium and they had indeed 'done a Glazers' and had loaded debt on to the club. Like a politician going back on an election pledge, the owners had hoodwinked their electorate. The 2007 arguments started the alarm bells ringing for many long serving Liverpool fans. One of them was Peter

Hooton, lead singer with the pop band The Farm, and an intelligent and passionate advocate for his club through his writing and frequent media appearances. Well connected and influential, Hooton, who did his share of activism in the 1980s, knew it was time to take a stand.

I met Hooton in the Twelfth Man pub near Anfield before our Europa League match against Lille in March 2010. Amid his detailed critique of Liverpool's owners it wasn't difficult to detect anger and defiance. "The writing was on the wall when Benitez had a fall out with (the owners) in the summer of 2007," Hooton said. "Bear in mind he had just taken us to two Champions League finals in three seasons and if 10 years ago you had said we would do that you would have been taken away by the people in white coats. There was a honeymoon period with the Americans and then the rumour went around that they had no money. It was a rumour at the time, but then there was the fall-out with Benitez and then they went around lining up other managers such as Klinsmann. We were tipped off by a few journalists who said 'look this is serious, they have had meetings and if you want Rafa Benitez to be history let them get on with it, but if you want to do something about it – the time is right.'

"That was November 2007 and it was a pro-Benitez march and then we became aware of the debt on the club just after Christmas. There was a network of Liverpool fans' groups from websites and fanzines who all decided to have some sort of crisis meeting."

That meeting took place at the Sandon pub near Anfield, another place steeped in LFC history as it was here that the club was first formed by publican John Houlding. "No one knew what was going to happen,"

Hooton recalls. "A lot of the established fanzine people were hoping it would be a loose network of fanzines and people who ran coaches to away matches. But what happened was unprecedented. It was like an old trade union meeting – 300 to 400 people; all vociferous and all passionate about Liverpool Football Club. That was the catalyst and no one knew which direction it would go. There was a steering committee early on but it was totally fluid. Anyone could join it and anyone could leave and in the early days that is exactly what happened. I made a few phone calls to people I knew who had been active in the Labour Party in Liverpool during the 1980s and one, Paul Rice, had chaired Broadgreen Labour Party which was a difficult thing to do. So I thought if he can chair Broadgreen Labour Party he will be able to chair a meeting of 400 football fans because a lot of messages were going round on the internet saying it will turn into a rabble, I said 'trust me, I have got someone who can chair this.' "Paul chaired the meeting, reluctantly by the way. I said 'the club needs you, Paul and you have got to do something.' So he chaired it and did a magnificent job. Various people came forward to get involved. After the steering committee was set-up and we saw who was involved we knew it could be high profile and we needed to get it properly organised and we went down the legitimate route which costs a lot of money."

In the early days the new movement was known as Sons of Shankly, but there were complaints about male bias and so Spirit of Shankly was born. The group immediately knew it could expect detractors and so was keen to prove everything it did was legitimate and transparent. It established sets of aims, pledging to represent the best interests of Liverpool FC and hold the owners to account. It promised a fair deal for fans, to build relationships with supporters all over the world and to promote regeneration in Anfield, an area that has been blighted by housing problems, crime and deprivation. The Electoral Reform Society oversaw elections of committee members.

Hooton said: "We wanted to do it above board with the ERS involved and we wanted people elected. We said anyone can stand for any position and we don't want this to be a closed shop. Even if you have ideas which are totally opposed to ours you are still welcome. Come into the committee, argue your case and you might change opinions. Ever since then it has been an elected committee and people involved on a day to day basis. Sometimes you might miss a couple of days and you come back to find 200 emails. It's unbelievable. It puts paid to that lie that young people are not interested in politics because this is politics with a small p. The older ones like myself decided to take a bit of a back seat even though we will do interviews. It is for the younger ones because we have seen the glory days and all that and we are doing it for future generations. People on the administration side are putting a lot of hours into it. Everyone appreciates the people who are doing the admin because without them the whole thing would collapse.

"It is a very new organisation and unbelievably it has 5,000 paid up members and another 20,000 on Facebook as followers. It is a massive commitment, getting £10 off football fans, believe me. Even though they will pay £30 or £40 for a ticket, getting £10 off them for an organisation means there are 5,000 very committed. On the marches before the Man United game in 2008-09 there were 4-5,000 on those marches and they were fantastic. Obviously marches are not going to stop carpet bagging businessmen but it does tell them they are not welcome and that's why we have started the 'Not Welcome Here' campaign and we will be a thorn in their side. Really the writing was on the wall if you had Googled them. I wrote an article for a local magazine when they first took over and I sat on the fence and said 'let's see what happens with these two' because one was a friend of Bush and you are not a friend of Bush's for your charitable works. I was very dubious but I didn't realise the nightmare scenario we would be in now. Bill Shankly used to say this is about natural enthusiasm and the one thing you can galvanise is people's love of their football club. A lot of people don't understand that because they don't understand how people invest most of their life in their football club, people who spend thousands of pounds each season following Liverpool.

"You got two people coming in who wore scarves when they first came here and made the right sound bites but people soon saw through them. It is a purely business decision from the type of people who might asset strip or just go for what they can get out of it. It could be baked beans, or famously Weetabix, another leveraged buy-out that Hicks that was involved in."

Hooton mentions politics frequently in our discussion, but for Spirit of Shankly this has the potential to be a weakness as well as a strength. As a city, Liverpool has long had a reputation for being a centre of struggle and protest. Some Liverpudlians argue this been harmful to its reputation and economic standing and there are clearly

LFC fans who don't care for the alleged socialist tinge of the SOS rhetoric. One regular on the Liverpool Echo message board, petersmith, was scathing of the SOS after the July 4 rally and wrote: "When I went to the ground as a boy it had nothing to do with politics as it didn't for all the supporters and it still doesn't for 99.9% of fans. Kick SOS and its politics out." Others condemn SOS for being 'pseudo militants.' A counter-revolutionary Facebook group called 'Sick of the Spirit of Shankly' has been set-up.

But if the methods were open to debate, in the summer of 2010 no-one was arguing with the sentiment of Spirit of Shankly's Hicks and Gillett 'Not Welcome Here' campaign which has been taken up by fans all over the world. Other banners derided the Americans as 'liars and cowboys' and a poignant message came from The Kop: 'Built by Shanks, Broke by Yanks.' Off the pitch, nothing was what it seemed and relations between the club and fans reached depths that none of us could have predicted. For example, towards the end of the 2009-10 season, a new chairman, Broughton, was appointed, whose role was to flog the club on a "willing seller, willing buyer basis". A former chairman of British American Tobacco and a Chelsea season ticket holder, his cold demeanour and unconvincing statements of reassurance made him an easy public target for the Kop. A new public enemy also emerged in Christian Purslow who was accused of undermining Benitez and stoking the fires of discontent behind the scenes. A drip feed of damaging stories continued to fill the front and back pages often seemingly fuelled by damaging media briefings by public relations consultants. It emerged that Liverpool lost more than £50m in the financial year to 2009. It was also reported that a staggering £22.3million had been spent on the new stadium that wasn't. For the second year in a row, independent auditors KPMG suggested there was "material uncertainty which may cast doubt on the parent company's ability to continue as a going concern." In other words, LFC were skint. It was widely reported in the spring of 2010 that the club were forced to give assurances to the Premier League and UEFA that we would be able to fulfil our fixtures in 2010-11. To my knowledge no one at the club has denied this in which case it would be one of the most humiliating episodes of all.

None of this was a surprise to Tomorrow's Company, a UK-based charity and a limited company which focuses on the role between business and society. In 2009-10 it researched the 20 Premier League clubs of the time and produced its own league table of stewardship. Tomorrow's Company defines stewardship as "handing something on to the next generation in better shape than you inherited it − the active and responsible management of entrusted resources, taking account of the interests of stakeholders now and in the longer term." And where did Liverpool feature in the Premier League of stewardship? In the relegation zone. Nineteenth, in fact. Tomorrow's Company was blunt in its assessment of the club. "Big debts...feuds between owners have unsettled manager who manages in spite of, rather than supported by, the owners...stadium not sorted out." They did at least put us a place clear of Portsmouth in the stewardship table.

Outside Merseyside, some of the greatest anger towards Hicks and Gillett is expressed by their fellow countrymen. New York based journalist Jim Edwards, who was born in Fazakerley in Liverpool and grew up in Heswall, said: "The mood runs from mere embarrassment to active dislike. Saying there would be no debt and then it turning out there would be debt that has soured everything they have done. I really think if they had been honest it would have been different."

In fact Tom Hicks junior, a son of Tom Hicks and a one-time director whose public relations skills extended to abusing a fan in the notorious "blow me, fuck face" email, prompted much controversy during a brief time as branch member of the New York supporters' branch. Branch chairman Daragh Kennedy said: "He came into the bar, sat down and watched a match with some of his mates and never identified himself. Apparently he was wearing a Texas t-shirt. He signed up to join the club and there were those on the committee who were outraged by that and thought we should do all sorts of things. I am a bit more diplomatic and I don't believe in having emotion when you are making decisions like that. My personal mindset – and this is me talking not as president of the (supporters') club – is 'I may not like them but they are going to be the owners of Liverpool for some time and I am not going to do anything to spite myself.' I wanted to play the political angle on this and we all feel the same way about the owners and the broken promises, but I don't think we all know the full story and I will reserve judgement until the thing is played out. But the committee were not of that opinion and they were outraged. We did write to him (Hicks jnr) asking what is the story and what his intentions were. We never got a response." Needless to say Hicks is no longer a member of the branch.

Looking back to Moores' fateful decision, could DIC have made a better fist of ownership than the Americans?

For some, any alternative would have been preferable, but economic crisis in the Middle East had a serious impact in 2009-10. Bob Kabli, from the Dubai branch, said: "To me it is almost embarrassing that the Liverpool name is touted cap in hand around the Middle East or wherever. It goes against the whole Liverpool way of keeping things in house. Most supporters wouldn't care who owns the club as long as there is some continuity, some consistency. It seems in general that there is as much interest in what is happening off the pitch as on it. A lot of people have made a lot of money for doing not very much over the last 10 or 15 years. It is difficult to say whether it would have been better or worse under anyone else. There is the passion out here and I know DIC did genuinely have an interest and supported the club, but you could argue they would want more day to day involvement. For us it would have been brilliant as we would have had more links (with the owners)."

The more you read about Liverpool's ownership issue the more complicated and bewildering it is for those who are better with league tables than balance sheets. As this book went to print it was hard to know what unhappy turn this tale would take next. Broughton, who frequently reminds us he is a 'part-time chairman', knows just how tarnished Hicks and Gillett are. In an interview with *LFC TV* he deflected questions asking whether there would be more representation from fans on the club's board in the future. But he did use a revealing phrase in stating that new owners must understand the 'ethos' of the club, a coded criticism of the current ones, no doubt.

In August 2010 a proposed takeover by the Asian owner Kenny Huang broke down and there was media speculation – subsequently denied – that LFC might be effectively foreclosed by the banks. As the main creditor is RBS, a bank largely owned by the British taxpayer, this suggested Liverpool FC could be effectively nationalised.

Whoever owns Liverpool by the time you read this, what the last few years have shown is that things cannot be taken on trust any more. In one respect, it is wholly appropriate that the fans' union is named after Shankly as he had his run-ins with directors until he found some he could trust at Anfield. A genuine grass roots, match-going fan has to be right at the heart of any future decision making. We need to demand genuine influence for the dedicated fan, not patronising comments and commercially driven spiel about us being the '12th Man.'

Meanwhile, Peter Hooton has ruled himself out of a future seat in the Anfield directors' box. He told me it just wouldn't be his thing. So he will continue to campaign from the grassroots and he might have to give up a few more Sundays getting involved in the Spirit of Shankly's city centre protests. Hooton would be delighted to see a proper Liverpool fan on the board 'as long as he isn't a patsy.'

In April 2010, Hicks and Gillett announced their 'intention' to sell the club and they issued a statement which was truly shameless. "Owning Liverpool Football Club over these past three years has been a rewarding and exciting experience for us. Having grown the club this far we have now decided to sell the club to owners committed to take the club through to its next level of growth and development."

The question for Liverpool supporters is just how much more of this 'growth and development' can we take?

16.

From fans to consumers

"They (young people) are learning how to be Liverpool fans from Andy Gray and I don't think that's acceptable." **Alun Parry, co-founder of AFC Liverpool**

When I was about eight, one of my most played records was 'We Love You Liverpool We Do' by The Kopites. The vocalist, in unapologetically Scouse tones, spent three minutes celebrating the virtues of the 'mighty Reds of Europe.' Thirty-odd years later, that scratched piece of seven inch vinyl is still around, safely tucked away in a wardrobe at my parents' house. I also have a copy downloaded on to my iPod which is a neat reminder of how times have changed in the music industry as well as in football. But back to the song. I was always envious of The Kopites because they got to sing Liverpool chants in a recording studio. How great must that have been?

One man who knows is Ian Abraham, who is Liverpool's voice of the Number One fan, a football themed novelty with a difference. Unlike most merchandise which is based on the players, Number One Fan celebrates the role of the supporter. The toys have been created to resemble your typical supporter dressed in club colours and sporting a beer belly. The Number One Fan sings some of the best known songs heard on the stands of his favoured team. They retail for £19.99 and, naturally, Liverpool is among the best sellers.

Ian's brief was simple – sing your heart out for the lads. He said: "It was a brilliant thing to do. We went to the studio and there were two other guys there and I was given some money and asked to pretend I was on the Kop. I stood there and I remember thinking I have to do this properly to justify this man's cash and I belted the songs out with gusto. The song they most liked was 'We are the famous, the famous Kopites.' I did 'You'll Never Walk Alone' obviously, 'L-I-V-E-R-P-O-O-L,' 'Fields of Anfield Road' and 'When the Reds Go Marching in'." LFC approved all the chants which had to be non-current, non-player specific and clean – which narrowed the choice considerably.

Ian watches Liverpool home matches in the Main Stand and said: "I have not really mentioned it to the guys at the match but when Tim Lovejoy featured it on Sky I got some texts saying 'that's not you, is it?' I own two (Number One fan toys) and I occasionally I do get it out of the box and say 'you'll never guess who this is? Especially to a friend I haven't seen for a while. There is a 'positive reluctance' to show it to people. I was a bit pissed off that the fan had a beer gut! But I do genuinely like this doll and I am quite pleased to be affiliated with it because it is done by football fans for football fans. It looks good and if I am honest most fans do have a beer gut. It is probably a case of vanity on my part. I like what it (Number One fan) stands for and it is a very good design."

Like all the best ideas, the concept was sketched out on a beer mat by Paul Jeffrey, an Aston Villa fan and graphic designer who, with his business partner Ian Clifford, gained licenses from LFC, Man United, Chelsea, Arsenal, West Ham and Spurs. There is also an England Number One fan (hopefully, minus the irritating brass band). Abraham, who worked on design projects with Jeffrey in the music business, was brought in as an authentic Liverpool fan to make the singing realistic.

Jeffrey said: "The idea came about because football fans have a lot of merchandise, but we wanted something for the fans of 35-45 with beer bellies who love their team. The Number One fan is modelled on the typical family member who is a football nut and his family and friends will look at the fan and say 'that's our Frank or our Stan.' It is all about the fan. We have been on a lot of forums and what comes across is that people take football far too seriously, but this is just a bit of fun."

If Number One Fan is the benign, slightly portly shape of football supporting, the onward march of aggressive commercialism shows no sign of easing up despite the economic downturn in the UK. In the chapter on money we looked at the potential £4,000 cost of travel and match tickets and it was stated that this didn't include many spin-offs. If the football fanatic really wants to follow everything going on at LFC and he or she buys all the publications related to the club – match programmes, weekly magazine, *The Kop* monthly newspaper, fanzines etc and also takes out subscriptions for the e-season ticket on LFC.tv, ESPN and Sky Sports –- there will be little change from an additional £1,000 for the season to match day costs. Replica shirts, scarves and a whole shop full of other goods can be added to a potentially infinite wish list.

When Ian Ayre took over as Liverpool's commercial supremo in 2007 his brief was to bring clearer focus to LFC's revenue streams. And many people reckon the Merseysider took on one of the toughest jobs in football. For years there were grumblings that LFC had sold itself short. "We are one of the biggest clubs in the world and yet we can't get the marketing right," was a common complaint by critics who said that LFC failed to properly capitalise on its unique reputation. This criticism was noticeable even – especially – after the miracle of Istanbul in 2005. Ayre, an expert on marketing and media rights in Asia, has already had a strong influence on commercial operations at Anfield. Whatever we might say about his bosses, Ayre is not a man to be underestimated. We have already seen a new food court on Anfield Road, posh club stores in the city centre and a commercial partnership with Thomas Cook which is controversially selling match tickets through travel packages. There are mobile beer sellers serving us lager from backpacks. Who knows how many other cunning plans Ayre has on his flip charts? If threats to boycott club merchandise in 2010-11 in protest against Liverpool's ownership are backed up with action, he will need to be even more imaginative in prising cash from fans.

One of Ayre's more welcome ideas is a very simple one which is long overdue at Anfield – asking the supporters for their feedback. These days, website surveys are common on LFC.tv and towards the end of the 2009-10 season I received two phone calls from friendly, customer focused ticket office staff asking for my opinions on the new admission policy for members which means entry to the ground is now via a fan card and a mobile phone text message which confirms the seat number. After 30 years when the club didn't know who I was, they can now trace all my buying habits and they have an archive of all the matches I have bought tickets for. It is strange that while the absentee landlords wreaked havoc off the pitch and took fortunes out of the club in chaotic circumstances, the commercial strategy was changing before our eyes.

Whether that is a good thing is another matter. One of the charms about supporting Liverpool in years past was the club always kept commercialism at arm's length. True, we were one of the first English sides to have shirt sponsorship, but we were one of the last to have perimeter advertising, or a scoreboard and we have never gone in for dancing girls, razzmatazz, mascots or any of that bollocks. You went to Anfield for the match and even our DJ George Sephton is unique, 'the John Peel of Anfield' as he has been dubbed.

Even when it came to keeping the sponsors happy it was all done with a slightly embarrassed air. Crown Paints had the good fortune to sponsor Liverpool in the 1980s and before home games on the pitch they displayed a huge paint pot that was divided into two parts, dismantled and carried away by stewards 15 minutes before kick-off. After a while this strange branding exercise became just another odd little match day ritual.

It was during Crown Paints' sponsorship that I first experienced the double edged sword of commercialism. For the 1984 League Cup final replay against Everton at Manchester City's old home of Maine Road, my dad managed to wangle a couple of seat tickets from a contact at work. We later learned that the tickets, which were gold dust to Liverpool supporters, were being casually passed around as freebies to friends of the sponsors, not all of whom could be bothered to go. Scandalously, on the night there were empty seats in our section for a match of key importance to Red and Blue alike.

Much has changed since then and commercialism has taken a grip that we never could have imagined in the 1980s. It is widely acknowledged that the game is more fan friendly in some ways since that troubled era. Facilities at grounds are in a different league for instance. Not so long ago, saying you were a football fan in some circles of English life was tantamount to an admission of thuggery. Things couldn't stay as they were, but Paul Jones, a Liverpool supporter, writing on *The Times'* Fanzine Fanzone blog in 2009, made some well observed points about the nature of modern Premier League football. So well packaged, so expensive and nothing like as much fun. His comments are worth quoting at length.

> Jones wrote: "The move away from supporting to spectating is the one change in the game I resent the most. Several decades of cleansing by the authorities in a move to stamp out hooliganism and tribal fandom have achieved sanitisation of the game and shut out the next generation of supporters. The moves that have taken place within our game have rendered fandom an endangered species. The fans now filling these grounds are also reflective of their designs. Identikit fans only wearing different colour shirts. Singing the same songs as every other side, just replacing the name of the club they support. They dress the same, they act the same and they have fallen for the great whitewash of falling in line; doing exactly as the

authorities want them to. The clubs play loud music over the PA for them to dance and sing along to and they lap it up. The same happens in countless grounds in all divisions, and takes away the opportunity for each group of fans to impose their own characters and cultures on the club."

Of course Jones' favourites can never just be "an identikit team". Clive Tyldesley, a TV commentator and Manchester United fan, worked as a radio commentator on Merseyside earlier in his career and knows the club and its traditions well. During the 2009 Champions League quarter-final between Chelsea and Liverpool at Stamford Bridge, Tyldesley made reference to the notorious plastic flags given free to the London club's followers to generate an atmosphere. "Liverpool bring their own flags," said Tyldesley, who, in five dismissive words, showed the fundamental difference in the two clubs.

But even good old fashioned Anfield loyalty and traditionalism has been under attack. As we have seen elsewhere in this book the all-seater/members only/online sale with a credit card model of getting into the ground simply isn't appropriate for many fans. Priced out, forced out, the casualties of the Premier League decided that if they couldn't get into Anfield they would bring Anfield to them.

The result was the formation in 2008 of AFC Liverpool which described itself as a "new independent football club owned by Liverpool fans where everyone can buy into it and get an equal vote. A genuine grass roots, not for profit football club. It is aimed at those Liverpool fans priced out of Premier League football.

Same colours, same songs, same community of Reds."
That's where the similarities end as AFC Liverpool play
in the Vodkat League Division One otherwise known
as the North West Counties which is eight leagues and
several hundred million pounds below the promised
land of the Premiership. It is here that you see football
in the raw with uncompromising defenders, sharp
elbowed strikers and shaven headed midfielders
given to shout "come on, ay, lads. We're going quiet."
This is no place for Alice-band-wearing-Fancy Dans.
There is little talk of diving or 'simulation' at this level
as the players get properly kicked and don't need to
fake it.

For some this is a throwback, a reminder of the days
when you could pay a few quid to get in, chat to the
players and felt like you belonged. AFC Liverpool don't
have their own ground and have to share with
established non-League team Prescot Cables. The
ground isn't actually in the City of Liverpool itself and
the club would like to put that right if and when they can
find a suitable site. Some wonder why AFC Liverpool
was founded in the first place, couldn't the fans priced
off the Kop have simply followed one of the established
non-League clubs in the area such as Marine, Bootle or
Prescot, indeed? The club respond to this on their
website, stating "being a football fan is about belonging
and partisanship. If anyone has partisan feelings towards
an existing non-league side then you will already be in a
position to follow them too. But most LFC fans have
only ever supported LFC."

Unlike AFC Wimbledon or FC United of Manchester,
AFC Liverpool is not a protest club. It was born as
discontent against Liverpool's owners began to rise on

Merseyside, but the non-Leaguers are proud of the support that their big brothers gave them when the club was set up. Quotes of support from Kenny Dalglish and ex-boss Rafa Benitez are prominent on the home page of the website and John Aldridge, who was a non-League and lower league legend himself before finding fame at his beloved Anfield, said: "I love the idea that Liverpool supporters now have our own non-League team."

AFC Liverpool lost 2-0 in a dreary clash against midlands side Eccleshall when I saw them in March 2010. The next day I was at Anfield for one of the happier memories of a desperate season, a 3-0 win against Sunderland. There were 135 fans for the first match and 44,000-odd more for the second. The idea that AFC Liverpool can be anything other than an interesting sideline for Reds fans isn't disputed, but for one man the launch of the new venture meant a break with a lifetime of support for LFC.

Local fan Steve Fraser saw the future before most of us and didn't like it one bit. He was dismayed when the Tom Hicks and George Gillett takeover was announced and vowed that 2006-07 would be his last season following Liverpool FC. This was no easy pledge for a season ticket holder who followed his club home and away. But he has kept his promise and these days divides his time between two hugely contrasting football venues – Valerie Park and the Nou Camp, Barcelona where he is a member and takes in about 10 home matches a season.

At each home fixture at AFC, Fraser displays his banner "red and white, not stars and stripes", but three years on does he regret turning his back on a football team that was once such a big part of his life? "It was a hell of a shock but I had about three months to get used to it because there were about a dozen games left after the takeover. I used to sit in the Upper Centenary and the more I looked across at the directors' box and saw them, the more I grew out of it. It didn't seem that strange even when the last game was the European Cup final (2007). The first game of the following season was strange but that is only to be expected I suppose. I thought it would be difficult and they would put the club into debt, but I didn't think it would be as bad as it was. Mine was a point of principle on the ownership. I suspected they wouldn't get the stadium built, but I wasn't certain that would be the case. They (Hicks and Gillett) have absolutely ruined it. You can't have a football club in that situation and they have got it to the stage where if they miss the Champions League two seasons running they probably won't get back there for the foreseeable future.

"It was amazing because after Heysel and Hillsborough people asked me if I would pack it in and I never did. Then when I did pack it in all the people who you thought might say 'great, you've finally got a life' were all quite shocked about it. They were trying to talk me out of it. I am always a decisive person and once something's done, it's done. I didn't have AFC to support the first season because it was the year later they came in. I wasn't too sure what I was going to do but I was an associate of Barcelona and used to go to one game a season so I thought I would go to one a month. But when you are used to going to football you don't do one a month, do you?"

Fraser admits he has a different take on AFC Liverpool than his fellow supporters. "When it was first set-up the whole idea was it was a club based around Liverpool supporters which suited me fine. The songs were the same and the fans the same. I didn't know what to expect and I thought it might turn out to be bigger than it has. The reason it hasn't is because it isn't a protest club. I am the only one who sees it as a protest, nobody else does. I just enjoy the camaraderie of it. The away games are a good laugh and we generally have more flags than the other side have fans. It is a good day out. The cost is fantastic as a season ticket here is £70, but I didn't stop going to Liverpool because of the cost. You spend £10 in a day with AFC Liverpool, but then I might spend £300 the next weekend going to Barcelona. You can have a laugh and chat with the players and although it will take a while to grow to the level we want to be at it is still enjoyable."

But surely there must be a twinge of regret, a longing to get back to watching LFC? "No. It has dropped off. The season after I stopped going I always knew when the games were and I watched the games on TV. But gradually that changed and now half the time I don't know when they are playing. I made a point of watching them if I was in Barcelona, but I don't do that now. Certain games I will watch if there is nothing else on, but I found when the Champions League matches were on that I picked the game I fancied watching rather than Liverpool. I might keep an eye on (a Liverpool game) and hope they win, but I am not going to spend my time watching. As the time has gone by I am less and less involved which I thought I would never say, but those are the facts."

It is clear that Fraser enjoys the quality of football as well as the grassroots experience. That explains his new commitment to Barcelona. Fraser said: "I was first interested in Barcelona because of their history (a symbol of Catalan nationalism and opposition to the dictator Francisco Franco). I particularly liked the fact that Barcelona is owned by the fans, by 170,000 members and we all pay 155 Euros a year which works out at about £30m for everyone and that is the ownership structure. I get to vote for the president and you feel a part of it. It is a comedown to realise that you don't get every ticket you want because at Liverpool I had every one guaranteed. At Barcelona it is one ticket per member and everything is a ballot. So you put your application in online and you have the same chance as everyone else. It can be good and it can be frustrating as well." (Later in 2010, it emerged that Barcelona's off-field affairs were not in such great shape after all with stories of massive debts and players being paid late although they still found the millions to lure Javier Mascheranho away.)

There is always room for fans at non-League grounds and that is one of the reasons why Fraser was attracted to it when AFC Liverpool was formed. "The appeal is it is always 3 o'clock on a Saturday, you can always get in, you don't have to pre-plan, you just pay your fiver on the door and you can have banter with everyone, up to and including the linesman. You realise they can hear every word you say and they will come back at you. Much as we want to win, it is not that big a deal if you don't as you still enjoy it. I would say to anyone 'come down and watch some of these games'. We need to get out of this division because the league above has better supported clubs. The key thing is to get into the city (of Liverpool) because persuading

500 people to come out here every couple of weeks is difficult."

And what about AFC Liverpool's endorsement from the Anfield aristocracy? Did Fraser welcome the high level backing? "We all thought that was a good thing at the time, but I think it has minimised the support. FC United grew on the back of a protest and good luck to them as they have done a good job and were helpful when AFC Liverpool was set-up. The Liverpool FC support is great but it (AFC) is not going to grow on that basis and it needs to get its own support from within the community and if you want to watch non-League football in Prescot you have got your own team who have been here for 120 years."

For Alun Parry, co-founder of AFC Liverpool, the setting up of a non-League club was an important statement of principle. Parry, a musician who has since stepped down from direct involvement on the board but remains a fan, was adamant that AFC should be inclusive in all respects. "The whole point of this club is it is owned by the people as everyone is a member and has the same vote as everyone else. It is run on a democratic basis and that speaks to some of the issues at 'big Liverpool' if you can call it that. A lot of people thought at first 'you are like FC United, you are turning your back on Liverpool' and it wasn't like that at all. It wasn't even inspired by Hicks and Gillett although that is around. What we are doing speaks to some of the ambitions of Spirit of Shankly and Share Liverpool.

"If there was a political issue for me it was more (Premier League) game 39 (proposals) and the idea that football was eating itself to such an extent that the whole integrity of the competition was up for sale. If you consider the young kids they are learning how to be Liverpool fans from Andy Gray and I don't think that's acceptable. Everyone is getting the same thing. Liverpool, Aston Villa…we all have our own songs and our own heritage and that has to be expressed from the grass roots and not Tim Lovejoy on Soccer AM. That is not acceptable for the communities football represents."

17.

Arriverderci Anfield?

"If the new ground is ever built and I walk out of Anfield for the very last time it will be a very emotional time. I have spent some of the happiest days and nights of my life at Anfield and there are some fantastic memories."
Les Lawson

At some time in the next decade Liverpool Football Club may well have a new home. Now that might not appear to be the bravest of predictions. After all, the club has planning permission to move and everyone knows that the naming rights for the new stadium are up for sale. But any Liverpool fan who has been following the ground move story will argue that given the funding problems and the antics of Tom Hicks and George Gillett there is a greater prospect of finding the lost city of Atlantis than a shining new stadium a few hundred yards away from the old one. So any scoffing from you regarding this chapter is understandable. And yes, a comment of "I will believe it when I see it" is merited, but if you could suspend disbelief for a moment, let's imagine we could be set to move. How will it feel?

For some, the move from Old Anfield to the brave new world on Stanley Park will be a fresh start. It will offer the club the chance to fulfil its potential and earn more money to eventually reinvest into the playing squad. For others, it could mark the further loss of heritage and the risk of Liverpool playing in just another characterless ground with an even greater, crippling debt.

Wherever you stand, it will be a sad day when we say our goodbyes to Anfield. Manchester City and Arsenal are two of the biggest clubs in the country and each of them moved from their traditional homes to new stadiums in the last decade. Liverpool's move will have more in common with Arsenal's in that the removal vans will only drive a few hundred yards and not several miles across town as is the case with City.

But – famous as Maine Road and Highbury were – the news stories that marked the last games on those grounds will be nothing compared to the coverage on the day when an era ends on Merseyside. It will be a day raw with emotion and memories of too many great games to mention.

Anfield was of course home to Everton from its opening in 1884 until the great split of 1892 when Liverpool Football Club was first formed. It has staged tennis, rugby league, community events, pop concerts and even a sermon by the American preacher Billy Graham in its time, but of course it is synonymous with the history and achievements of Liverpool Football Club. And of course the 12,500 capacity Kop dominates the ground just as it did when it was a 30,000-capacity terrace. There are many famous stands and terraces in world football but none is better known than Liverpool's Kop.

If a newspaper as stuffy as the *Daily Mail* can name Anfield as the most atmospheric ground in the history of football as it did in 2008, then we must have been doing something right over the years. For me, the current Anfield is too ingrained in my football psyche to ever lose its power. We could move to the most modern, space age stadium; we could win the league every season and we could all drink free ale each match brought to our seats by beautiful women and some of us still wouldn't be happy. We would still leave the New Anfield after a 5-0 win over Manchester United or Barcelona and reminisce about the days when Shankly saluted the fans, when the Kop sang along to The Beatles or when St John, Hunt, Keegan, Dalglish and Gerrard humbled some of Europe's finest teams.

A ground move has been discussed seriously for at least a decade. By the dawn of the new millennium it was obvious that while Manchester United were progressing on and off the pitch with trophies and extensions to the towering stands at Old Trafford, Anfield was stuck in a 45,000 capacity time warp. To make matters worse, by the time Gerard Houllier was bringing silverware back to the club in 2001, many fans were unable to get tickets for home matches. Like Highbury at the same time, Anfield seemed to offer 20th Century solutions to 21st Century problems. Arsenal got their act together and moved to the Emirates Stadium, an impressive piece of architecture but nothing like the club's former home which had lots of character.

Since 1992, the ground changes at Liverpool have resulted in a new Centenary Stand to replace the old, smaller Kemlyn Road area. The Kop was of course made all-seater in 1994 and an extra tier was added to the

Anfield Road End in the late 1990s. But while the ground remains a dramatic stage for football, its capacity is simply too small. Sad as it may seem, there is a feeling that while the old Anfield is a backdrop for a glorious past, it cannot be part of the future.

John Pearman editor of the fanzine *Red All Over the Land*, is a self-confessed traditionalist, but even he understands why relocation is needed, if the money can be found. "I can remember when they first mooted a new ground and the feeling was 'never.' There was a group called Anfield Forever. But now you won't find anybody that says we should rebuild Anfield. The feeling is we have to have a 60,000-80,000 stadium somewhere – and the sooner the better. If Liverpool had looked at it more closely about 15 years ago they could have rebuilt Anfield. Whether they can now, I don't know."

Norwegian Liverpool fan Anders Gustavsson who studied for a Masters Degree in Social Anthropology at the University of Oslo, spent time with many Reds fans from Merseyside finding out their opinions of the club in 2008-09. One of his research questions looked at the issues of a ground move – and the findings were not what he expected. "I was a little surprised because most of the fans want to at least have a bigger stadium and as long as it is not possible to extend the stands at Anfield Road it seems like they want a new stadium so they can get more revenue to compete with the best teams in England and Europe. The importance of winning things seemed to be greater than staying at Anfield Road. I think maybe just moving to Stanley Park is important on this issue because you can continue your match day rituals. It is really the same area."

But as with everything in modern football it's all about money. The Liverpool Daily Post's business editor Bill Gleeson looked closely at the figures in March 2010 and concluded that a £300m-£400m ground could add up to £3m per match in terms of revenue. Admittedly this was based on a lot of assumptions (a 75,000 capacity and everyone paying a lot more per head), but it did give an indication of how much LFC are losing out now by not having a bigger ground. Gleeson spent most of his article analysing in detail just how capable Hicks and Gillett might be of raising the funds to buy the stadium and the conclusion was: don't hold your breath.

Publicly, the pair always said a new ground is top of their agenda and blame global economic forces for delaying the building work. But by the summer of 2010 they were clearly lame duck owners who were desperate to sell. It was inconceivable that there would be any real progress with the new ground while the Americans remained in charge.

On his takeover in February 2007, Gillett promised Liverpool fans would have "the greatest facility in this sport", and pledged "a shovel in the ground in the next 60 days or so". In fact, if you go back to Gillett's quotes and read what he actually said it was more carefully worded than that: "If we are to preserve the grants — and we are extraordinarily appreciative of the community grants – the shovel needs to be in the ground in the next 60 days or so." So really was it more about maintaining the grants and keeping everyone on board rather than getting on with a project that we all now know they couldn't finance anyway?

The Spirit of Shankly group later staged a Greenpeace-like picture stunt when their members donned high visibility workers' jackets and performed a ceremonial dig in Stanley Park when they had lost patience with the owners' ability to get the building properly underway.

Even if Liverpool had been taken over by two ethical can-do businessmen with money to finance the project, 2007-08 would have been a rough time to build a ground as the banking crisis and rising steel costs cut off lines of credit and forced material costs to rise. As early as the summer of 2008 Gleeson wrote in the Daily Post: "Never is a big word, but it is extremely unlikely that Liverpool Football Club will build a new stadium at Stanley Park or anywhere else for many years to come."

Eight years earlier, Rick Parry, who was still new to his job as chief executive, feared that Liverpool FC could "stagnate" if they were unable to bring in more match day revenue. Crucially, at that time, the club decided that it was impossible to extend Anfield given the fact that the ground was hemmed in by terraced streets, some of which have since been demolished in regeneration projects. Ten years ago, The *Daily Mail's* John Edwards offered a tempting prospect of what could lie ahead for Liverpool in the Eldorado of a new ground. "If he (Parry) can push through his most visionary and ambitious proposal of all, Liverpool's return to the top table of English football would be just about complete," Edwards wrote.

Three years later, plans were submitted and the cost at that time was estimated at £80million for a 60,000-seater ground. There were also ambitious plans to transform the area around the ground that had long been plagued by poor housing, rising crime and social problems. There were complaints from local residents who were concerned at losing Stanley Park, a public amenity, to a commercial organisation, but overall it seemed too good to be true. After stumbling their way through the early years of the Premier League, Liverpool FC at last seemed set to modernise their operations and bring in a lot more money.

But the whole project became bogged down in disputes over funding and feasibility studies. A proposed ground share with Everton kept resurfacing in the press only to be shot down. By 2006, the estimated costs had soared to more than £180m and despite saying his dream was to lead Liverpool out at a new stadium, Rafa Benitez wondered whether it was possible for the new ground to reproduce the passionate atmosphere of the old one. History showed that Rafa need not have worried about a ground move as when he left in June 2010 little had progressed. Every so often during the noughties, plans would be presented online and in the press, but the more the subject was discussed the less likely it seemed that it would happen. Liverpool's new ground is consequently 'on hold' in much the same way as my family's plans for a 20-bedroom holiday home in Monaco are.

It is a tale of missed opportunities, broken promises and poor strategic leadership. We were left with the farcical situation of a large part of Stanley Park cordoned off ready for a massive building project that didn't look as if it would happen. For Peter Hooton, pop singer, writer and Liverpool supporter, the stakes are big for the club and the local residents who have been left in planning limbo. Hooton, a leading light in the Spirit of Shankly Supporters' Union, is not alone in wondering if a fresh approach is needed to the whole subject.

He said: "What has happened to this area (L4) is an absolute disgrace and it is almost as if there is this beacon of wealth in the middle of a very deprived area and it is scandalous really. We (SOS) have community links as well and obviously we are not going to dictate to the local people what we want but we will say 'we are there if you need us'. We were involved in talking to Keep Everton in Our City and had a meeting about the football quarter. We have seen the plans for a redeveloped Anfield. It looks fantastic and would cost £200m. According to the architects and builders it is possible."

A ground move might appear pie in the sky, but if it does happen it could address the nagging issue of Liverpool's ageing match day fan base. Some fans believe a new Anfield would enable those who have been priced out of going to the match to be welcomed back. There are even suggestions that a section for youngsters could be brought back. A new age Boys' Pen, perhaps?

Anil Patel, of LFC's Herts branch would welcome any such initiative. "If I could change one thing it would be to make it easier for local people to get tickets, particularly youngsters, otherwise you will lose the next generation of fans," he said.

For London-based Scouser Ian Abraham, there has already been an adjustment of sorts as he has switched a place on The Kop to a spot elsewhere in the ground. "I have a season ticket in the Main Stand with my wife although she is 20 rows in front of me and you tend to find that singing in the Main Stand is just not de rigueur. I suppose am over 35 now so I sit with the old buggers in the Main Stand. They are a good bunch and at half time I join my wife and listen to the guys behind whose analysis of the game is excellent – you learn something all the time."

Les Lawson, secretary of the Merseyside branch of the LFC Supporters Association, can see the logic of a move to a new ground although his feelings are inevitably mixed. "If the new ground is ever built and I walk out of Anfield for the very last time it will be a very emotional time. I have spent some of the happiest days and nights of my life at Anfield and there are some fantastic memories." But Lawson was keen to emphasise the significance of the word 'if' in his comments above.

Football never ceases to surprise and there is a chance that an investor could be set to turn the new ground proposals from pipedream to reality. Sure, it will be painful to see the bulldozers going into Anfield. But we are wise not to confuse talk, speculation and boardroom pledges with action. The bulk order of Kleenex for Liverpool 4 can wait.

18.

Remembering the 96

"There was a blanket put over Hillsborough and that blanket has got to be removed." **Margaret Aspinall, Hillsborough Family Support Group**

Each year on April 15 a group of Liverpool fans in South Africa pay their own tribute to the 96 supporters who died in the 1989 Hillsborough Disaster. They gather at the original Spion Kop, once a Boer War battleground that gave its name to the famous terrace at Anfield, and is now a national park in KwaZulu Natal.

"We follow the timeline of the events that happened in 1989. At that time of year we are one hour ahead of the UK. We meet for lunch at 1200 and then we talk about what happened and the aftermath," said the event organiser Guy Prowse.

"We drive to Spion Kop for a memorial service. One of our members speaks through a whole breakdown of what happened. To have eight or nine people on a hill in South Africa singing 'You'll Never Walk Alone' has a totally different meaning, a different emotion. Just before 3pm (UK time) we read out the names of the 96 who died and we then have six minutes of absolute silence. Then we sing the 'Fields of Anfield Road'. It is immensely moving."

Prowse and his fellow Liverpool supporters feel it is the right thing to do. At first it was an informal way of remembering the tragic events of a warm spring day in Sheffield, but now it has developed into something much more. Fans travel from as far away as Cheshire to be a part of the commemoration. They want to pay their respects and also hope that one day the authorities will have the decency to provide the families of those who lost loved ones a full and honest account of what really happened a generation ago.

Prowse said: "There is an invisible umbilical cord linking a hill in KwaZulu Natal to the greatest piece of stadium anywhere in the world. They share the same name and that is hugely, hugely important for us. We go through the history of Hillsborough. My kid was born in 2000 and he was up in Spion Kop with me for the memorial and he can tell you, without much prompting, a pretty good description of what took place and why we talk about justice.

"A lot of South Africans wondered why we kept talking of the need for justice and it is sad that there are some fans who display apathy. But there are younger fans who are not apathetic at all. We are two hours from the hill from which the Kop was named. It felt right to gather on the 15th and the first one was a case of a couple of guys talking about what happened. In 2008, we decided we wanted to make it a real memorial and commissioned a bench. It was done by telephone calls and emails and we didn't want to do anything that diminished the tremendous respect we have for the 96. We spoke about a permanent memorial and our tribute.

Spion Kop is a national monument in South Africa and we were not allowed to put anything there. But right next to the hill there is a hotel and they agreed to house a memorial. We wondered what felt right and we didn't want a cold thing, a stone with engraving. Obviously all-seater stadiums came out of Hillsborough with the Taylor Report. We commissioned a bench made of Rhodesian teak with is very durable, a beautiful natural wood and we have two eternal flames on either side because as much as we remember Hillsborough we would never forget Heysel either. The bench is made up of 96 individual slats and the back has two Liverbirds."

Sheffield April 15 2010, morning

Six thousand miles away, as Prowse and his friends are preparing their tributes, I am in a car approaching the home of Sheffield Wednesday Football Club. Driving past places with names like Oughtibridge and Grenoside, I see the ground emerge on the South Yorkshire skyline. It is always a shock when you see the facade. I have been back there about five times since I stood on the Leppings Lane terrace for the abandoned semi-final against Nottingham Forest and always feel tense as I see the terraced houses near the ground where fans queued in strangers' homes to phone home after the worst disaster in British soccer history. Too many painful memories, too many reminders of all that tragedy and suffering. On closer inspection the ground hasn't changed much in 21 years although the Leppings Lane terrace has long since been replaced with seating. In 2010, Sheffield Wednesday announced plans to modernise the ground in a £22m development plan which would mean rebuilding the stands which back on to Leppings Lane. (Whether the plans will have to be scaled back after reports of more financial uncertainty at the club emerged in the summer of 2010, remains to be seen). From the outside, it all looks much the same as it did at 2.30pm on April 15, just about the time when things started to go so horrifically wrong.

Much has been written and said about Hillsborough: words of fact, of powerful emotions, of heroism and words which attempt to make sense of the terror of that day. An interim report and a final report into the disaster by Lord Justice Taylor looked for causes, explanations and told football that it needed to move to all-seater stadiums and make dramatic improvements to crowd safety. Taylor's reports told the world what all of us who were there knew to be obvious – a failure of police control caused fans to be crushed to death on the shallow, overcrowded standing area behind the goal that was being defended by goalkeeper Bruce Grobbelaar.

A small but vocal minority of armchair cynics occasionally voice ill-informed opinions about what went on in Sheffield. These prejudiced, vested interests have, over the years, in the words of Trevor Hicks who lost two daughters at Hillsborough, "tried to rewrite the Taylor Report". They have attempted to complicate what was a very straightforward event by blaming the Liverpool fans. This rag tag band of attention seekers and know nothings range from tabloid editors to TV producers, radio shock jocks to government ministers and local councillors. Their views are always misguided, always hurtful and based on a basic misunderstanding or callous disregard of what really went on. Needless to say, none of them was at the match. None of them saw what I, and thousands of others, saw.

When I was still a journalist in 1999 I spent 10 minutes on the telephone correcting a reporter from Turkey who had heard this propaganda and was adamant that hooliganism was to blame. I felt it was my responsibility – not just as a Liverpool supporter but as a human being – to tell him that Hillsborough was all about a failure off police control and crowd safety.

Sadly, some of the people with skewed opinions also live in Sheffield and have fallen for the smear stories. In 1999 a survey found that despite the findings of the Taylor Report, 59% felt the Liverpool fans were to blame for the disaster and not the police. That was the same year that Wednesday allowed *The Sun* to sponsor the home game against Liverpool in an act which beggared belief.

A memorial to the 96 was eventually put up at Hillsborough, but it is on the main road away from the ground and you have to search for it. On April 15 2010 I spent a few minutes starring at the scarves laid in tribute – from Celtic, Plymouth Argyle and others – before I felt I had to get out away from the place and leave it to its redevelopment. History has shown that answers are not forthcoming in Sheffield and to bring some understanding to this tragedy you have to drive 70 miles west back to Anfield which was the focal point for the mourning in 1989 and has hosted an annual memorial event ever since.

Anfield- April 15 2010, afternoon

"It's our 21st – but we're not celebrating" read a t-shirt worn by a fan in the car park behind the Main Stand.

This was the 21st memorial at Anfield and although the attendance was down on the massive 30,000 12 months previously, The Kop was full.

At Anfield there was a procession from Walton Breck Road to the eternal flame with fans walking solemnly and carrying banners of solidarity. Heads were bowed and at the Shankly Gates scarves from clubs all over the world showed that it isn't just on Merseyside that Hillsborough is remembered. Some wore funeral suits, others preferred replica shirts and there was no shortage of Evertonians in the crowd. I also spotted a Manchester City top. Genuine football fans from all over the world feel an affinity with us on April 15. Deep down, all fans of a certain age know that in 1989 when supporters were turnstile fodder with few legal rights, it could have been them. This is backed up by a chilling video clip I saw on YouTube which was taken from ITV. It shows crowd congestion from the 1981 semi-final between Tottenham and Wolves at Hillsborough when fans had to escape the Leppings Lane End.

The 2010 memorial service itself followed a familiar theme with hymns, and readings including one from former Liverpool striker, John Aldridge who was deeply affected by Hillsborough and its aftermath. As in South Africa, the names of all 96 victims were read out and it was achingly sad to realise just how long that took. There was also a brilliantly performed Hillsborough related song, 'Tragedy', by Lee Roy James and choruses from local choirs. Again, the fans on The Kop sang 'You'll Never Walk Alone' and 'Justice for the 96'. There was a dignity about the protests and it felt strange to be on The Kop more than 20 years after some of us were there in the immediate aftermath of the disaster when flowers and scarves filled the terraces and the Anfield pitch. I will never forget the smell of those flowers and the tears of the fans on the Kop in the days after the disaster.

Somehow, there was a feeling that maybe – just maybe – the 21st memorial service could yet prove to be one of the most significant of all. In 2009, the then Sports Minister Andy Burnham was left in no doubt about the strength of feeling from the crowd. As Margaret Aspinall, chair of the Hillsborough Fans Supporters Group said, Burnham listened to the anger and demanded of his government colleagues that something should be done.

That something was the formation of the Hillsborough Independent Panel which was going over a mountain of evidence never previously made public as this book went to press. The panel's brief was to consider all the information related to the disaster. The panel includes The Right Revered James Jones, Bishop of Liverpool and veteran TV presenter Peter Sissons who are currently working their way through two million documents.

There was widespread concern on Merseyside in the summer of 2010 when Jeremy Hunt, the Culture Secretary, raised the issue of hooliganism when he compared Heysel and Hillsborough in a cack-handed attempt to suggest how well football has done in ridding itself of hooliganism. Hunt apologised, of course, and assured us he had not intended to offend. Some despaired, others wondered if Hunt had really been careless or was it all politically motivated. After all, the Hillsborough Independent Panel was set up by the Labour Government but some feared it might be less of a priority for the Conservative/Liberal Democrats coalition in these difficult economic times. The Government later assured worried Liverpudlians that the panel was safe and that its work would continue as planned.

The years since Hillsborough have been marked by a succession of cruel false trails and attempts to cloud the issue and dilute public sympathy for the Hillsborough families. No wonder many wondered: was Hunt's comment merely the latest obstruction of justice? But if the panel can shine some light on the darkest corners of the Hillsborough files, they will have done everyone a huge service. As Margaret Aspinall, who claimed not to be a polished public speaker but delivered a very moving and inspirational address at the 2010 memorial, said "a blanket was lifted over Hillsborough after the disaster and now it is time for that blanket to come off."

The families of the 96 have always known who their friends are and those attending the memorials are told that they have played a vital role in keeping the pressure on those who would prefer that the uncomfortable facts of 1989 were kept hidden. For the guilty ones, confusion and controversy are a useful safety net. Liverpool Football Club nailed its colours to the mast with a strap line on the official website on April 15 2010 of Justice for the 96, echoing the battle cry of the campaigners. In addition, the *Liverpool Echo* consistently championed the cause of the families even when the national press lost interest. That same paper displayed its coverage of the event from 1989 publicly on display boards in the reception of its city centre offices near the waterfront and when I was there I saw a number of fans of my age in quiet voices explaining to their children some of the background to these cuttings.

So let's hope there is a breakthrough in the fight for justice. I remain optimistic that Liverpool fans are not going to let this matter rest until that blanket is lifted. This was made even clearer to me by seeing so many young people at the 2010 memorial. This was remarked on at the service and it is a strong point which reflects well on the city of Liverpool. The Hillsborough tragedy features on school syllabuses and campaigners and survivors have provided first- hand accounts for pupils who have been educated on what really went on. As I was leaving the ground after the service I heard two lads – just ordinary Scousers in their late teens or early 20s – talking about what they had heard. Maybe they were just babies at the time of the disaster but it was clear that for both of them it remained important.

This reflected a feeling that young and old will not let this matter rest until we reach the end game which has to be a genuine sense of justice and clarity for those affected. The families strongly feel they have been badly wronged. Any fair-minded person would agree and surely it is not too much to ask that they be treated with some long overdue respect. "We are the eyes, ears and voices of the 96," say the Hillsborough families.

We must do all we can to support them.

—⁓—

Among Liverpool supporters who were born in the city, everything is up for discussion and debate, with one exception – *The Sun* newspaper. When I was setting up an interview with Richie Greaves who runs the Scouse Not English website he was very friendly and helpful but I told him I was an ex-journalist and before he agreed to talk to me he wanted to establish that *The Sun* wasn't on my CV. Another Liverpool fan wears a t-shirt with the message "I have seen Billy Liddell, Tommy Smith and John Aldridge. I don't buy The Sun." Anil Patel from Middlesex was born outside Liverpool but takes a harder line than some on Merseyside in that he won't allow *The Sun* or the *News of the World* on the coaches he books to travel north to Anfield.

At each game at Anfield you see stickers reminding fans to have nothing to do with the country's highest selling daily newspaper. The TV comedian Alexei Sayle proved that you literally could not give it away in a stunt for a series of TV programmes filmed in the city of his birth. Ryan Babel had to issue a statement through the Liverpool FC website in the 2009-10 season to clarify that he hadn't spoken to *The Sun* and nor would he when an article appeared there speculating on his future. Graeme Souness, who went from legendary midfielder to pariah during a disastrous spell as manager in the early nineties, now realises he was fortunate to escape the sack for selling his story to the newspaper. A few years ago I used to chat to a guy who emptied newspaper recycling skips on Merseyside. Murdoch's red top was rarely seen.

Scousers are often criticised by the rest of the country for having a chip on their shoulders, of insularity and of harbouring grudges. Others acknowledge that Liverpool fans deserve praise for sticking to their guns and not allowing an historic injustice or a 'disgrace to journalism' as the *Liverpool Echo* put it, to be forgotten. This stand has come at a price for some. One fan who lives in North Liverpool told me his relationship with his brother, an exiled Scouser with a shorter memory, has been damaged. It deeply saddens the fan that he has to remind his brother not to bring the paper to his house.

In this book I have tried not to preach and there are times when I have edited out personal reflections, but in this case I hope readers will allow me a few moments on the soap box. It is difficult to know what goes through the mind of someone who spends time and money following Liverpool, buys merchandise, sings 'You'll Never Walk Alone' and still buys *The Sun*. But you do see those who describe themselves as a Liverpool fan with it. I spotted one the day after a game in January 2010, in a Liverpool replica shirt proudly showing off near Lime Street station, oblivious to any offence he might cause or the example he was setting to the young lad he was with. In 2007, my late friend Steve Rooney and I were waiting to board a ferry to Athens from one of the Greek islands on the morning of the Champions League final when there was some idle talk at the quayside and a group of fans from the Merseyside area were reading a tabloid newspaper next to us. A south east based 'Liverpool fan' who we had got talking to the previous day before we knew his reading habits piped up in all seriousness "Is that *The Sun*?" – in a tone of interest and certainly not contempt – before he realised what he said, thankfully out of earshot of the other group. Steve and I shook our heads and found somewhere else to sit on the boat. This was a fan who could trot out endless trivia about Liverpool players and must have known about the boycott as he allegedly sat on the Kop and went to all the away matches.

Can these people really have missed those 'Don't Buy the Sun stickers?' *The Sun* has no place in the hands of Liverpool supporters, local or otherwise. An Irish

Liverpool fan wrote to *The Kop* newspaper on this subject, urging all supporters to boycott *The Sun*. *The Kop* made a good point which was that the sort of Liverpool fan who would read *The Sun* wouldn't take *The Kop* anyway.

Long before Hillsborough, celebrated eighties Scouse lifestyle fanzine *The End* called *The Sun*, "the empty heads' favourite newspaper". But it did sell on Merseyside until April 19 1989 when it published a front page with The Truth splashed on it together with allegations that Liverpool fans robbed the bodies of the dead at Hillsborough, urinated on corpses and hindered rescue attempts. These allegations were described as smears – which is putting it mildly. In the years since the coverage in *The Sun* there have been some who reckon it's about time that Liverpool fans "moved on" and learned to forget about what was said then. "Today's reports, tomorrow's fish and chip paper," as the saying used to go. *The Sun* has tried and failed to reach an agreement with the fans to bring the boycott to an end.

In fact one newspaper *was* forgiven for its coverage of Hillsborough. The *Daily Star* published many of the same claims as *The Sun* but it backed down when it realised that the claims were fiction dreamed up by South Yorkshire Police and the Conservative Party. As a result the *Daily Star* is widely read on Merseyside and *The Sun* isn't.

Over the years I have occasionally been unlucky enough to hear some non-Liverpool fans tell me that they know better than I do and that "there was something in the Sun's story, you know." It doesn't seem to occur to them that I was there and they weren't. But anyway, consider this. In 20-odd years, millions of words have been written about April 15, 1989. Many rightwing journalists with an agenda would have been delighted to discover a smoking gun which proved that crowd disorder and not police incompetence was the cause of 96 deaths. Many of those journalists who know every trick in the Wapping book spent hours door stepping, digging, stirring. And what have the newsrooms come up after all this time? A risible, contemptible story in a hysterical newspaper that was discredited before it was printed. Sadly, this newspaper is a cancer that goes deep into British media life. It remains very powerful to politicians, celebrities and others who either don't know or don't care that when editor Kelvin McKenzie libelled a set of football fans and an entire city he caused wounds that never healed.

The reality is that there isn't and never was a smoking gun. If it hadn't have been for the quick thinking of Liverpool fans the death toll would have been higher. There are Liverpool – and Nottingham Forest – supporters who literally saved lives on that awful day by giving first aid. The Hillsborough cover up began the moment the first football fans died as a result of police operational failures. When everyone accepts this without qualification the better it will be for British journalism.

It is also unfair and unwise to simply accuse out-of-towners for not respecting the Hillsborough families and breaking *The Sun* boycott and it is important to remember there are many non-Scousers who are on the right side of this argument. I spoke to Americans and South Africans who have barely set foot in Liverpool yet feel almost as strongly about this than many of us do. These dedicated international fans sometimes get sent web links from other "Liverpool supporters" alerting

19.

The Future

"I am an ex-player and an ex-assistant manager but overall I am a fan and I hate seeing the club in the mess it is in at the moment." (**Phil Thompson, quoted in the** *Liverpool Echo*).

The future has rarely seemed as uncertain as it does now for Liverpool Football Club and its fans. I spoke to countless Reds who knew exactly what they wanted to see happen at their club – sensible ownership, significant team investment, increased ground capacity and new facilities either on the present site or on Stanley Park. But when it came to discussing what they thought *would* happen the situation was nothing like as clear.

Among Liverpool supporters there is a school of thought that suggests we are traditional club which has never truly got to grips with the Premier League. We were in the unfortunate position of being the club with most to lose when Sky and the FA introduced a whole new ball game in the early 1990s. We had been the dominant power in the English game for so long that in 1990 our 18th and last league title was treated with a degree of complacency that is embarrassing 20 years on.

In understanding where we are now, we have to return to pivotal years immediately after that last league title win. Back in 1990 we had an ageing team and a manager in Kenny Dalglish who was forced to deal with stress and health problems which were surely largely related to the Hillsborough disaster. Dalglish's resignation in 1991 was on a par with Bill Shankly's departure 17 years previously in terms of its shock value. It also wrong footed the club completely. By 1991 we were also approaching the end of the ban from playing in European competitions which was a result of the Heysel tragedy. It was also a time of change in the boardroom and we needed an evolutionary manager, a Joe Fagan for instance. Instead we got Graeme Souness. The Scot's judgement was poor and his apologists' claims that he "was a winner who couldn't stand others not having the same passion as him" should not be taken seriously. Souness recruited sub-standard players and alienated himself from his players and the fans with his behaviour. His decision to sell his story to *The Sun* was simply the most extreme case of rank bad management.

It was no surprise that after Souness's ill-starred tenure at Anfield ended with a humiliating FA Cup defeat to Bristol City, Roy Evans, a completely different character and a boot room veteran, was appointed in an attempt to calm shattered nerves and reassure us. Evans did a lot right and built an entertaining side, but he lacked the defensive organisational skills and the ruthlessness needed to succeed as a manager and was forced into a bizarre job share with Gerard Houllier before leaving the club altogether in 1998.

Off the field, the early 1990s featured the building of the Centenary Stand and the last days of terracing on the

OUR LIVERPOOL

Kop before it became all-seater. The boot room was demolished as well to make way for a new press room. Anfield was changed forever.

In 1995 I was journalist watching from the press box when Blackburn Rovers were crowned champions at Anfield on a glorious May Sunday. Blackburn's triumph was at Manchester United's expense and how they laughed on the Kop and enjoyed the reflective glory of seeing Dalglish hold aloft the silverware. It was a surrogate title for some Reds and yet that day now seems a watershed moment in the English game. Not for Blackburn's emergence (they never achieved such heights again) but for the power of new money. Chelsea and Manchester City symbolise a lot that is bad with the modern game, but most of all they demonstrate that, to paraphrase my favourite band The Jam, you can't do nothing unless it's in the pocket.

Cash is an unromantic fact of life about 21st Century football, as we have seen in this book. Cash to get to matches, cash to pay for TV subscriptions if there's no room for you at the ground. Cash to pay mediocre players fortunes in the hope they will blossom in the future. Cash to service stratospheric debts. Cash for merchandise. Cash, cash, cash.

And yet Liverpool supporters – whether there really are 100million of us or not – do not begrudge handing over money. It is found for all the season tickets, travel, away trips and European matches. Money is available to make banners, to launch supporters' branches, to join the All Red membership scheme. Over the past two decades football has severed many of its historic links and for fans so wrapped up with tradition as Liverpool's are that has been painful. Fans would happily pay the money if they were able to, but many have been frozen out, lost to a game that has been gentrified.

The Kop, a monthly newspaper which has a fan's perspective on matters at Anfield said in a comment article in the September 2010 edition: "…it is Liverpool's loyal, traditional working-class fan base who are paying the price. They are the ones who are increasingly finding themselves edged out of Anfield, leading to a very real sense of bitterness about how their loyalty has been repaid by Liverpool…"

Liverpool FC has always been part Scouse club from the back streets and part international sporting phenomenon. This contradiction used to concern me. Around the time of the Athens European Cup final, I feared that these two sides of Liverpool were irreconcilable and might lead to serious and damaging tension among our different types of fans. Three years on the stakes seem far bigger and the debate is not just about ticket allocation and the changing face of Liverpool's support.

Now we have moved on to a different landscape with vital questions to be answered. What kind of a Liverpool FC we will support in coming years? Who will be the supporters of tomorrow to follow those who grew up worshipping Shankly, Paisley and Dalglish, arguably the three most celebrated figures in Liverpool's history? Where will the money come from to satisfy our ambitions? After the bruising experience of Rick Parry, David Moores, Tom Hicks and George Gillett, who will we trust to run the organisation that is brilliantly summed up in six words on that massive banner we see at every home game on the Kop: 'Our Club, Our Crest, Our Life'?

The answer to the ownership question seemed as elusive as ever at the end of August 2010 and it is an issue the club simply have to get right after the shambles of the last three years.

If this book has thrown up more questions than answers, that's typical of the times we live in. Naturally, whatever happens, we will carry on singing the old songs and keep the faith even when results are not what we had hoped or another signing fails to deliver. We have taken a number of wrong turns that have stifled our progress on and off the field. We long for LFC to get back to what it always did best – winning trophies and attracting ambitious, talented players with a point to prove and the character to perform in front of some the most knowledgeable and demanding supporters in world football. We could definitely do without another season like we experienced in 2009-10 when we were eliminated from four competitions and failed to finish in the top four.

Ours is a club of myths and legends, triumphs and victories in the most unlikely circumstances. It is a club rich with characters on the field, in the dug outs and in the stands, if not in the directors' box. When it really matters, no fans get behind their team like ours. Often this club has brought us joy, sometimes our support of it has been tested to the full and occasionally we have experienced tragedy with it. For a long time we have had supporters all over the world and many of them are exiled Scousers who have spread the gospel.

Wherever this story is heading next, we will be there, fans from all five continents, watching at the ground or on a TV screen. After all this is, was and always shall be, Our Liverpool.

The End

20.

Acknowledgements

My first and biggest thanks must go to my wife Lucia and my children Anthony and Ella. They have put up with me throughout the research when I regularly said "Please keep the noise down I have to interview someone on the phone." Lucia has offered me detailed suggestions on how to improve the content and Anthony has made a lot of helpful comments on how I can make passages clearer.

My father Tony also had a massive part in this book as he took me to my first game in the 1970s. My mum Jessie always used to say when I was a kid that "I hope you will grow out of football one day." I think she has given up on that now. Thanks also to my sister Ally who remembers when my LFC mania was at its height in the 1970s and 1980s.

I have been helped by dozens of people who are quoted in this book. They were patient and willing to talk at length about their love of Liverpool Football Club, a love that has been severely tested in recent years. A special mention must go to Graham Agg for his enthusiasm for all things Red and his tireless work in building links with fans of Borussia Mönchengladbach.

Graham has been very encouraging and his invitation to me to speak about this project at a Liverpool pub in Christmas 2009 inspired a lot of follow-up ideas and many contacts.

Peter Hooton of the Spirit of Shankly Supporters' Union was typically articulate and thought provoking with his thoughts on the future of the club and his comments were important in helping me understand a little of how SOS has developed from a grass roots protest to an effective lobbying group. Les Lawson of the Merseyside branch was encouraging and enlightening as were all the supporters' branches I contacted. LFC Boston got my research off to an excellent start by offering me stories, comments and one of their t-shirts.

Charlie Lambert, my colleague at the University of Central Lancashire, provided fascinating first hand insight into how the media cover Liverpool, and a range of blogs, websites and publications which have been referred to in the text were invaluable. Among them were the *Liverpool Echo, The Kop, Well Red, Tomkins Times, Red All Over the Land, Through the Wind And Rain online, OhYouBeauty, Red and White Kop, lfhistory.net and* many others.

Keith Salmon, author of *We Had Dreams and Songs to Sing*, was full of good advice, contacts, help and encouragement on self publishing. I must also thank the Liverpool fans who went on the friendship trip to Germany in April 2010 for their ideas. Among them were Ian Graves, who I also spoke to at the Independence Day event in Liverpool on July 4 2010, who was a great sounding board for some of my ideas which were discussed in an Irish bar at 3am! Lee Sprung was instrumental in putting me in touch with the New York branch.

As I wrote in the introduction, this book is in memory of Steve Rooney and I would also like to acknowledge Steve's brother James (or Jimmy) Rooney and his family. James gets to games with me whenever he can and it won't surprise you to hear that he isn't very keen on John Terry.

I can't let a book about Liverpool supporting pass without mentioning my late granddad Alec Bell who was a typical hard-to-please Main Stand season ticket holder who took me to see the reserves and, in the 1970s, told me football pundits didn't know what they were talking about. He was clearly ahead of his time there. My other match going cronies over the years include my best man Andy Richards and Paul Thomas who were regulars with me on the Kop in the 1980s. Rob Leslie, an Oldham fan who has been my mate for nearly 30 years, gave me some of the best advice in the summer of 2009 when he urged me to "keep it objective". He clearly knows what a biased, opinionated so and so I am. Thanks are also due to the Royal Mail lads past and present for their interest when we were on our annual winter jolly in Berlin this year.

Chris Brain's excellent picture is used on the cover of this book. Check out more of his pictures on Flickr. Ridhima and Clare of the Business Elevator (www.thebusinesselevator.co.uk) produced an excellent promotional video for me which you can find on YouTube – search for OurLiverpoolBook. I am grateful to all the people who have helped me make this book a reality. Many have improved the words I wrote and any mistakes are my responsibility alone.

LaVergne, TN USA
03 November 2010
203325LV00001B/19/P